Blossom &

Become

By Anna Garcia

Photography and cover layout designed by

First published 2017
831 Designs
London. UK
www.831Designs.com

Book Blossom and Become / Anna Garcia. -- 1st ed.
ISBN-13:
978-1973946762

ISBN-10:
1973946769

Contents

"The flower doesn't dream of the bee, it blossoms and the bee comes"

Dedication

This book is dedicated to the woman who has too often left it to others to decide who she is.

To the woman who after going through much pain has not lost hope in love and is set on creating beauty in her relationships;

to the woman longing to nurture the most meaningful relationship of all, the one she has with herself.

To the woman who recognises that when she blossoms, she becomes & the bee comes.

Thank you's

A big thank you to my mentor, Wilson Luna, who changed my world & that of many women through believing in my work and holding a vision for a journey much bigger than I could ever had imagined. For your love, belief & eternal patience.

To my dear friends and fellow speakers dedicated to shining a light to the world, in particular Chris Hill for inspiring me to finally give birth to my story in writing and to Warren Ryan for unknowingly bringing out the best speaker & coach in me.

To my mum & siblings who have supported me relentlessly and who have taught me the art of loving others for who they are and who they are not.

And finally, to all my soul family, friends, crew & participants, without whom this journey would not have been possible.

Thank you, thank you, thank you
From the depths of my heart.

Forward

Anna's book is going to amaze you, a true gem in the world of relationships, it's a love story from beginning to end, the love for a mother, her father's, her lovers, her siblings, it will break your heart and then repair itself, it's a story of one young woman's fight for identity, love, and compassion. It's going to make you laugh and cry, it's going to pull at your heart strings but most of all it's going to give you hope that no matter what happens to us in life there's always a way out, this is the first book where I've felt pain and then joy all at the same time, there's always a future even when we don't see it. Anna's ability to show this through her Latino ways are incredible, she is a true friend coach and mentor to so many and I feel reading this story is as real as yesterday.

Thank you Anna for sharing your incredible life story.

Chris Hill.

International Speaker, Number One Best Seller & Addiction Specialist

www.beatmyaddictions.com

CHAPTER ONE

When you Hit Rock Bottom

His fist was about to land on my cheek and as I screamed out his name in plea, he stopped, as if his arm had been jolted back by an angel. I'd reached rock bottom, alone and full of shame. But strangely, I also felt that I was being given another chance. In that moment I was able to realize that I didn't have to stay. As much as I felt responsible, I didn't have to be responsible for his life.

At this point we're in Colombia because he had been deported. He was an asylum seeker. He'd begged me to travel over to him. I was a student at the time. We'd spent half a week together and he demanded that I wasn't allowed to go and see my family who lived across the country. This one morning we'd got into an argument and as I screamed his name and broke down into tears, I said to myself, I don't have to do this anymore. I cried and I begged him, please let me go home to my family. He felt so guilty he let me go. I fled.

That would be the last time he would ever see me cry.

Up until this point my family didn't know that I was in an abusive relationship nor that I had been in one for about three years.

I got to my auntie's house and cried my eyes out telling her the story. All she'd known up until that point was that I had married a man out of obligation. Because I felt responsible for his life. Because he needed me to marry him in order for him to stay in the country. Prior to that, I stayed with him and cancelled the wedding three times. I was seventeen when I met him. I had been a virgin up until that point and within three months I got pregnant. I was too afraid to go to the doctors and ask for the pill. I was ashamed.

After having fallen pregnant with him, I'd learned that he'd left a partner and two children back home. Little did I know that very shortly I was going to be raising his eldest son, who at the time was two and a half years old. So there I was, seventeen years old, pregnant with a partner. Estranged from my family. I was staying with an auntie at the time. She'd insisted to him that we needed to set up a home together. Around that time his mum came over with his son and they were staying in a hostel. They were asylum seekers. He thought it a good idea to have me go and live in there with them. So, with a room in a hostel, where I wasn't supposed to be staying, it couldn't get any worse than this, but it did. It was such a turbulent family he belonged to. It was aggressive and violent and I saw many things that I didn't need to see. They ended up splitting and I was left responsible for this two and a half year old child.

So, we're in a hostel in North London, my partner worked all hours. At this time I was still at school. Yup, I was at sixth form college. It was the summer holidays and I was now heavily pregnant. I just remember every week we'd get a visit from the woman responsible for the hostel. She'd knock on the door and my stepson would want to run to greet them "Who is it?" And I would hold him back and hush him, "No, you need to hide, I'd whisper, frightened we'd get caught. "You need to hide because we're not allowed to be here. I'm not allowed to be here."

My pregnancy was extremely stressful. I was hiding. I was in a place I wasn't meant to be. The young boy had severe behavioural issues. I remember there was a Nigerian cleaner that used to come and clean the halls in the mornings and we became friends. She couldn't believe it. She used to insist to me in a very heavy Nigerian accent, "Ah- You have a british passport. What are you thinking. You're entitled to your own place, Anna." And, "What is up with this boy? He's crazy." The little boy used to throw tantrums and start throwing cutlery out the kitchen window, among other things, to say the least. I became very fond of him, however his Dad was so insecure and emotionally unstable having been abused as a child, that he became jealous of our relationship and he made things very complicated.

So I'm heavily pregnant. I'm desperate. I realise that the family that I was with, not married into at this point, but was living into, was a turbulent, abusive family as a whole. I remember stepping out of the hostel bath one day, which we shared with two more families, feeling desperate. I remember dropping onto the floor just holding onto the basin above me. I was crying desperately. How did I end up here? Pregnant, estranged from my family, living with a totally dysfunctional family, in hiding from the hostel manager and sharing a single bed in a basement room that often became flooded leaving us swamped to our ankles with slugs and a like. How on earth did this happen? In that moment I turned to God in desperation and I said such a powerful prayer; "God, please don't let my child be born into this family." I begged, "God, please, give me a second chance." Now I loved my child but I begged God, please give me another chance at this, at life. Please don't let my child be born into this family. That night as I lay my head to rest, I forgot that prayer.

Some months later I'd built the courage to go and ask for help and I was now in my own hostel. Every night I'd go to bed. I would draw the curtains. Every night I'd go to sleep on my own. It was one of those hostels where you couldn't have your partner or anything like that. So he stayed behind in the other one and I was now in my own place. Every night I would go to bed and my baby would wake me up in the early hours. Every day, kicking, she'd wake me up. One Wednesday morning however she never woke me up. She didn't kick me. My partner arrived to visit that morning and he was insistent on having sex. Here's one of the first moments in my life that I thank God that I never allowed him to bully me into what he wanted. He was demanding sex and I said, "No, my child needs me and I need to get to a hospital now." I was eight months pregnant. Reluctantly and begrudgingly he came with me, we got on a bus. We went to the hospital. For hours I was monitored, and four hours in, he left to go back to work. So he left me there. Within 15 minutes of him leaving, suddenly I had a whole medical team around me, all these people suddenly insisting that I needed surgery.

I was petrified. I was 18 years old. I was a baby. I was being told I was about to have a Caesarian section. Straight away they called my Uncles' partner, my Auntie who became my 'comadre' (Goddaughter's mother) as I was Godmother to her baby girl. I remember she was there within a flash. I just remember being held. Then the anesthetist, they put the anesthetic on and I remember just trembling. They tried to talk to me so that I could keep calm. That's when I learned that my first language was Spanish. I could no longer respond in English. Anyway, a few hours later, it seemed, she was out and it was silent. I didn't hear any crying. She was laid literally about a metre away from me to my left. They put her on a little bed. I could see her moving, I was struggling to look through the surgeon's and doctors. I was struggling to look at her. I was so dozed out with the anesthetic, I said to myself, you know what, you've got your whole life to look at her. Don't worry about it. And I turned away. Then they took me to a separate room. Within about half an hour a nurse came in and she said, "It's going to be 50/50." Then within half an hour after that she came back: "I'm really sorry."

In that moment I felt like it wasn't me that was receiving that news. My comadre ran off crying. She reacted immediately. In my case, however, I was just frozen and I was frozen for a very long time. I didn't cry for my child for quite a while. I would cry at other people's mourning and I would suffer at other people's mourning but I was to be in shock for at least a month.

18 years old, I've just lost a child, I've gone through a Caesarian section. My comadre had taken me into her own home. I'm completely lost, completely confused. And this I'm about to share with you holds a very powerful lesson.

I had a wound. The Caesarian section, within about a week got infected and I woke up one day soaked in pus. I was petrified, my comadre called the hospital and the nurse said, "Oh, it's just an open wound don't worry about it, she'll be fine." But my comadre insisted on taking me to the hospital. She grabbed a cab and we head over there. I remember it was a Russian doctor and she said, "If you hadn't brought this girl in, the infection would have reached her bloodstream and she would have died within an hour" she'd saved my life.

I remember learning such a powerful lesson

because I always listened to authority and just did as I was told. In that moment she went completely against what a nurse on the phone had told her and she went with her gut feeling. and that taught me a lesson for life.

So, I got together with him. Having been advised during pregnancy that we were supposed to get married in order to keep a father for my child, even after her loss, I felt committed to marrying him. But I knew that wasn't the right thing to do. I just knew that the relationship wasn't going to work. I think that's why I cancelled the wedding three times, even the night before the wedding we were fighting, almost pushing me down the stairs. But I did it anyway. It lasted a year. There's a saying that goes; "you can tell with breakfast what lunch is going to be like." And I still didn't get it.

The day I left however, he wasn't to lay eyes on me for another 5 years.

But I have started in the middle of the story, let me tell you how I got to this point in my life.

"The joys of life bring us pleasure,

the pains of life bring us growth

but each pain holds a lesson

and a gift."

The Gifts in a nutshell:

- You are not responsible for anybody else's life or happiness
- Listen to your intuition, it can save your life
- Know who you are and love who you are, otherwise you are vulnerable to being abused or taken for granted
- Tomorrow is not guaranteed look at those you love today and tell them how much you love them, today.
- Know that your deepest most heartfelt prayers may well be heard, even if you forget them.

Share with us where in the world you are reading from and what lessons you are getting?

Go on share your view:
www.facebook.com/RelationshipsIntensive

CHAPTER TWO

I just can't rely on men

I'm 5 years old, we live in a council flat in Whitechapel, East london, Mum, dad and my older brother G. One day I asked my mum; "Mum can I go upstairs and play in the terrace?" "Yes, but go check with your dad." So I went to ask my dad and he said no. The next thing? I see is, World War III break out between them and I'm just standing there in the middle horrified, thinking to myself "Oh my God, this is going to be the one that's gonna break them up and it's going to be all my fault."

Fast forward I don't know how long, I have this foggy memory of dad waking me up at like three in the morning. It would have seemed that he was drunk. I'm sleeping on the top bunk bed, my older brother's down in the bunk below. He's six years older than me. He doesn't seem to have awoken. My dad's crying at the door. There's lights coming through from the corridor. He said, "Your Mum's chucking me out." I look at him confused, upset, and at the same time angry to see him so impotent and so pathetic. It was in that moment I made a decision. I said to myself; I just can't rely on men. Although such an unjust decision, this belief would become the basis of my relationships with men for most of my life.

From that moment on, life completely changed and I just remember being babysat by my brother every night as my mum worked every evening cleaning offices. Because there was such an age gap, we never got on. I was just this annoying little thing that always got in the way of him and his friends. I craved for his love, validation and attention, but I was met with sarcasm and aloofness which marked me and set the tone for my relationship with my brother for most of our lives.

So bless my mother, she became a single parent, and I remember she used to work late. Sometimes she'd bring a bucket of KFC, and other times she'd quickly cook us something and I just never forget this scene where we're sat around the table and I just felt pain in my heart to see my mum arriving so late and feeding us. And she just looked sad, alone and tired, not present.

She dished out this soup with egg in it. I didn't

know what she'd created, but I couldn't have it. I just couldn't have it. My mum was under so much pressure and so much stress, she was forcing me to eat this soup. And my brother who was usually so spiteful, when she turned away, began drinking mine as well, to help me. Bless him. That was how bad it was, and he just drank my soup.

That was a moment that I'll never forget, where my brother had his moments of being my hero. I always longed for him to be my hero, but he rarely was, occupied in his now teenage world. He was often spiteful and had a remarkable ability to make me cry through his wit and sarcasm. He was the most intelligent person I knew, always quick on his feet and had the answers to everything it seemed. He was so different to me, he was cool, trendy, sporty and athletic. I always felt out of place; not good enough, not light enough, slim enough, today I realise I made this all up in my head because I never got the love from him how I wanted but instead was met with cold aloofness. It was just his way of coping with what he was dealing with in all of our transitions. Looking back, there were many times he had my back, like the times mum would send him to bring her famous oversized purple velvet belt with tassels to punish me with, my goodness that thing was horrendous, but very much of it's time. My mama being a real latina, had armament for every occasion, being a single mum, she wasn't going to let us get out of order. Mum had such a handle on hitting with flip flops too, I could swear they turned around bends after me as I ran from her. But on one occasion my mum was so mad at yet again some mischief I'd been up to, like cutting off the hair of her hairstyling model heads she used to practice on at hairdressing school, that as usual she shouted out to G to bring her the purple tassled beast of a belt, only this time the belt was nowhere to be found. It remained a mystery how there was no belt for me that night. It was only 20 odd years later that I found out through his wife that my brother threw out not one, but many belts out of our 6th floor window. Being so trendy, I can't imagine the purple beast lasted long on the council gardens downstairs before they got snapped up by some fashion aficionada. That was my brother and still is, he saves my ass and says nothing about it, and some things never change, to this day he still does.

I just remember from that moment always having a longing, and my brother became the person who was my greatest influence. It wasn't my dad, it was my brother, his opinion that was the most important thing to me. So however my brother dressed, I wanted to dress. Whatever shoes he had, I wanted to have. Whatever football team he supported, I didn't even like football, but I wanted to support it.

I would visit my dad every weekend and I was daddy's little girl. My older, teenage brother was into his football, friends and girlfriend, so wasn't very interested in my dad, except his pocket money is what I could tell from his infrequent visits whilst I was there every other weekend. This was my dad's constant complaint. "Why is your brother like this?" I remember always feeling guilty as if I had anything to do with it, but this is something I also learnt to do from a young age, sadly, to adopt other people's emotions and actions, I feel responsible for them.

I loved my weekends with daddy, he used to spoil me so badly trying to compensate for not being part of our lives on a daily basis I guess. I was about seven years old, and I said "Daddy I want a bottle." So he got me a bottle, he would put Ribena and milk in it, yup, it was delicious and I used to lay on the sofa drinking this while we watched films, we loved watching films together.

One day my brother happens to visit and dad

asked me in front of him; "Honey would you like a bottle?" In front of my brother?! I was mortified! I knew what was going to happen, my brother looked at me, and I looked at my dad with these big eyes, like "yes of course, but, doh! Don't ask me in front of my brother!"

"Honey do you want a bottle?" I'm like, "No, dad. Thank you. I don't want a bottle." And so there it was, my brother had discovered my weekend secret! And of course, went and told mum. Oh my goodness, that was the end of my bottle days and my brother knew that he'd just ruined it for me. But he wasn't the only guilty one, to be fair, I was forever putting my foot in it too with my poor brother.

So every weekend I'd go out with my dad and we'd go and do stuff like trocadero in leicester square and he'd buy me kilos of sweets that Id get through far too quickly, we'd go ice skating, cinema, visit friends. It was just him and I against the world until one day. This woman showed up. He came and picked me up from home as usual and there was this woman in the front seat. I was like "Ah, she's taken me seat!" Little did I know that this woman was soon to become my stepmother. She was a "friend" however, and we began to go out with her every weekend. So I now took the backseat, literally, and it felt like in other ways too, yup, I felt very jealous, she was 'a friend', but I kept my suspicions. There was some little thing that wasn't quite right. She was lovely, She was really, really nice. But daddy was mine. Why in the heck did I have to share my dad?

Then one day I noticed that their hands came very close, and I just saw the chemistry. I was only seven. That night at the end of the weekend, they drove me back home, as soon as the door closed behind me, I leapt into mums arms and wept inconsolably "Mummy, daddy has a girlfriend. My dad has a girlfriend!" Mum jumped on the phone to dad as soon as she knew he'd be back home and all I heard her say with her usual cold tone to dad was: "Listen if you've got a girlfriend you need to tell your daughter."

He came around mid week, which he never did. And we sat outside, we lived in a council flat in islington, North London, we sat outside on the metal chains surrounding the gardens and he put his arm around me. The sun was shining, it was starting to set. He said to me "Honey, yes, she's my girlfriend, but I want to assure you"... And Here's where my dad said the fatal words that changed my world forever, and confirmed my belief already about men. He said to me "I want you to understand that I love you both the same."....THE SAME?! What, hang on, did this guy just say; THE SAME?!

In that moment I felt like the world stopped on its' tracks, The clouds just stopped. I was so enraged in that moment, and as if by magic, the chain broke, literally the chain broke, and we fell on the floor and although this relieved me somewhat as it mirrored my emotions, I was furious, I couldn't believe what he had just said. He loves her the same as me and he'd been going out with her for a MONTH? Bless my dad. He never really was great at communicating, It just wasn't his greatest asset.

That was when, God love her, my stepmum was introduced into my world, very elegant, graceful, mature woman, multi-talented as well. It was very confusing growing up, I would spend every other weekend with them, and they were so different in the way that they raised me. My stepmother was not as emotional so she was a lot more, factual when she spoke. She occured as less sensitive, but she wasn't. My mum was a lot more emotional, loving, sweet and very endearing. Little did I know then however that as difficult as I found it to adapt to this new woman's ways as a kid, with her ultra healthy culinary delights I disliked, her over the top cleanliness and her sometimes intimidating no nonsense attitude, that she would become one of my best friends, role models and allies in adult life.

Around this time my stepdad came into the picture. So I now ended up with two mums, and two dads. Here's where it gets really interesting. My stepdad was part of the original group of friends with my parents, so he was a good friend of my dad's anyway. My dad and my stepdad got on really well. My stepdad was an electric engineer. He would fix my dad's stuff and it was very normal to have my stepdad around my dad's when I was there, etc.

People used to ask me, seeing it was the 80's, It was quite unique, you know, It wasn't that common for people to get divorced back then, and people would say "How do you feel about your parents being divorced, now you have these step parents? "And I'd be like, "Oh it's amazing. My birthday's, I have double the presents, and Easter, I get more Easter eggs, and Christmas is just fantastic." That's the way I saw it. I always considered myself to be very blessed. I came to love my step parents so much and was always grateful that my parents had put their happiness first and made sure they found partners they got on with. This enriched my life immensely as a child.

From the age of seven to twelve, my life was about weekends, every other weekend with my dad. It was a wonderful life. We lived very good years with my step dad. My first baby brother, J, was born, when I was eight years old. I adored him, absolutely adored him from the moment he was born and little did I know then, the journey he and I would embark on later in our lives.

In my parents choosing to divorce and finding love again, they were choosing for them, not against anybody else, and I'm eternally grateful they made this choice because it taught me to choose for me and my happiness too.

The Gifts in a Nutshell:

- When we make a decision like: 'I can't rely on men' we live our life trying to prove that theory, or at least our ego does. We seek love and validation but then reject it when it comes along. This is the ultimate yet universal self betrayal.

- We say we want love and healthy relationships, but we don't realise that over 90% off our behaviour is unconscious, so we may say one thing, 5%, but the remaining 95%, our undercurrent of limiting beliefs and programming is fighting against us all the time.
- The codependent- aloof dance is a common one between two of the 4 relationship types.
- The Co-dependent seeks wholeness in the other, Aloof doesn't trust and wants distance. They are attracted to each other because they validate each other's' limiting beliefs.

Share with others what you are getting from this, you never know it could really be the gift someone needs today.
Share with us Where in the world you are reading from and what lessons you are getting?

Go on share your view:
www.facebook.com/RelationshipsIntensive

CHAPTER THREE

The only risk is wanting to stay

At the age of twelve my Mum decided she'd had enough, and we were leaving the UK. She'd suffered from depression her whole life and felt that a lot of it had to do with being away from her family and her beautiful, sunny, vibrant home, Colombia.

My whole world got turned upside down, because my last thought of Colombia was seeing policemen with machine guns, and gun violence. I remember hugging my Dad as we said goodbye. He would never hug his little girl again, because the next time he would see me I would be a young lady.

So we left for Colombia, mum, stepdad & my baby brother. My older brother was starting uni so he stayed behind. It felt like he spent more time with his friends and doing his own thing as a teenager, so I didn't make it mean much at the time, but the oceans that were about to separate us would cause a raft between us that would later take almost a lifetime to close up again.

Very soon after arriving in Colombia I was in love with the place. A decade later, the tourism board would create a strap line in view of its violent worldwide perception that said: "Colombia, the only risk is wanting to stay" and that was certainly the case for me, these next few years here were to set my tone of vibrancy, leadership and passion for life. I had some of the most incredible three years, I learnt a whole new meaning of family, friendship and love.

That's when I met my first love, Daniel. I was 13 and he was the funniest, most outrageous 15 year old I had ever met, he was unapologetically colourful and loud. Mum played the role of disliking him because we spent too much time together in her opinion, she would complain, there comes your chewing gum again, always stuck to you! Dani guided my heart straight into my first symptoms of love and desire, I was only 13. One incredibly sunny day we went with a group of friends down to the river. Dani and I walked off into the woods and what seemed like a short time, was apparently hours, we followed along the riverbank until we found a big rock in the middle of the water where the river narrowed, we jumped on to it and held each other as the river gushed around us.. It was so pure and innocent and alive. We continued along the river bank until we came across an open, lush meadow, we ran through the high grass until eventually collapsing onto the ground, no one could see us for miles. I remember to this day what I was wearing, my favourite flowery shorts and tiny top, we held, we kissed for the longest time, our hearts raced as he held me in his arms and the sun bathed us. When we eventually found our way back to the gang they chuckled and teased saying we were wearing each others socks! We both innocently and quickly looked down to see if that was the case, only neither of us had ever taken our socks off, or our clothes for that matter! As passionate and explorative as our young love was, it remained innocent and Colombia kept me a virgin!

My friends and I had motorbikes which when we rode we felt free like birds in the sky. I enjoyed seeing every colour of green set in the landscapes of the luscious coffee region, the mountain ranges, rivers, thunderstorms and sunshine.

Everything was about to change however over the next six months, life would shock me with some of the biggest opportunities for growth and true gifts when I eventually came to see them as that, gifts.

The long six week end of year holidays were upon us and mum had had enough of how attached Daniel and I were becoming, I had no idea what she was going on about, but anyway, as annoyed as I was at her, she sent me away for the whole six weeks, the first half I would spend with my dad's family in the plains and savannas of the south, Villavicencio, where I found my love for sleeping on hammocks. Children and adults played and danced to the harp like angels, horses galloped into the sunset, oh and I saw sunrises of such orange and red intensity that extended for miles across the savanna. I have never seen anything like it since. She then sent me to Medellin, voted recently as the most innovative city in the world, to her side of the family, where every 'paisa' as they refer to themselves treats you like a long lost brother, ' mi casa es tu casa' is not what they say but what they embody and where no problem is ever more than a quick issue to get resolved, I've never seen a can-do attitude spread across a whole society like that.

I loved my time away and although I missed my Daniel, I began to see what my mum was trying to show me, a big part of my world gravitated around him! I saw how attached I was and actually how much fun I could have without him! Little did I know then that I was in a totally co dependent and attached relationship, the thought of having fun without him had felt kind of painful up until that point. I began to understand my mother's point; that my world was revolving around a guy, I had become a satellite around this boy, who I'd made my sun, little did I know that this pattern or choice of relating to a boy would lead to such pain in my relationships as a woman.

So for the first time at the tender age of 14 I was learning to be with myself again. I now realise how young I was when my codependence patterns in relationships began.

But this trip was set to start off an incredible chain of events. On my return one of Daniel's best friends sat me down and gave me the lowdown of his best friends' activities, it never occurred to me to ask why he was volunteering all this information but I sat patiently and listened to what was about to cause me intense pain, then anger and finally my first experience of vengeance. He went on to tell me that Daniel had two-timed me while I was away. Poor guy, apparently his teenage hormones kicked in during this time going teenage crazy and saw not one but six girls! This hurt so much, but his friend very quickly told me it was ok, I could always get my revenge on him. What?! This hadn't crossed my mind, I just sat there in disbelief feeling heartbroken.

But I listened in carefully to this guy's crazy plan. He went on to say: "it's very simple!" with wide eyes and excited voice; "find someone else you really really like, start seeing him behind Dani's back and then when you're really in love, you give Dani a kick in the ass and dump him just as he deserves!" Oh, and then he said as a last side comment; " I can be your humble servant if you wish me to be". I couldn't believe what I was hearing. This guy had stabbed his friend in the back to try his chances with me.

This was his grand plan?!!

I liked it. The falling for someone else and kicking ass bit yes, but totally not with him though. So the guy lost his friend naturally and for nothing but I eventually went on to find a lot of gain for me.

So this was the moment I got trained in cynicism; like that moment when the good girl goes bad in the films, my sadness and disempowerment got taken over by anger, courage and then passion. I knew the information this guy had given me was true and although it hurt so much, resilience was a strong part of me.

Interestingly enough, rewinding some months back, a young man walked into our pharmacy, I'd never seen him before. I felt the ground shudder underneath me, as I sat behind my Mum's desk, he looked at me with such depth and smiled, in that moment I knew I was in trouble. How could you feel instantly connected with someone you'd never met before? He was elegant, graceful, quiet and centred, quite the opposite of the boy I was in love with. JC was very grown up and mature because although he was still only 19 he was of the world, he didn't finish school, he worked with his dad's coffee agency, loved to ride horses as well as high revolution motorbikes, had a small child and had lived with his girlfriend, a fatally attractive combination for a young, impressionable 14 year old with boyfriend avenging intentions!

When JC and I got together, we knew it would be only a matter of time before I'd have to leave for the UK, we were only together three months before I left, but it was powerful, thrilling and full of excitement, especially because for the first month and a half I hid it from everyone, even my Mum and her new boyfriend.

Yes, Mum had separated from my step dad some time ago and Nando came into our world. He was the most loving, hardworking guy and I'd never seen my Mum look so young, beautiful and happy, I wish I could say I was delighted but I wasn't at that time, the truth is I was upset that life was changing so rapidly and this guy was quickly occupying more space in my Mum's heart every day. I was jealous, very jealous. But he was patient and paid a lot of attention to what was going on in my world, he was a great observer and soon enough got on my side. And this is who Nando would be in my life to this day, a dear friend, my second dad, a raving fan and someone I could turn to always.

In those days though, the poor guy had to work hard to win me over, he taught me to drive, he convinced my Mum to let me have a motorbike for my 15th birthday, something that became traditional there at the time and his presence made Mum happier, my ego hated to admit it, but this guy was making Mum so happy she was even almost liking Daniel now.

Sadly for Daniel, my first love, it was too late by this point, I was seeing JC behind everyone's back. A mother's intuition never fails however and it was very soon that she caught on. Having just found new love herself she had a newfound level of empathy and openness I had never seen in her before. She said honey; I know what's going on and I want you to come forward and share it with me, I want you to bring him home, introduce him and bring it out into the open. She said the following: " honey, when someone lands in your heart and in your mind, there's no force that can extract it". My Mum bless her, must have been mortified but she did the right thing, no matter how scared she may have been about her little girl, she knew that in the light she was safer than in the shadows.

JC was so courageous, I was literally trembling when I went to ask him that he should meet my Mum, his response to me as he held my shoulders in his hardworking hands was; 'amor, your Mum doesn't eat people, it will be fine, I'm happy to go meet with her'. Ahh, sigh, his manliness got me everytime. He had the word of one thousand men and yet he said so little. He was the mysterious, loyal type. I could count on him and I felt safe and protected. My little brother J and I hid in my bedroom with our ears stuck to the door as Mum and JC had the conversation. He was dressed so beautifully, with his cowboy shirt and boots in his jeans, just always so classy and held his ground so gracefully, always made me smile, makes me smile now to remember him. That day I walked out of the house hand in hand with him and my head up high as we walked through town, knowing this relationship as short as it was going to be, had integrity and Mum and my new stepdads' blessing.

The Gifts in a nutshell:

I wish Id known then what I know now about codependency in relationships and how it steals away our freedom and our sovereignty. Since then I've made a point of becoming aware of this, particularly when starting a new relationship. Whenever I find myself leading back into attachments, anxiety or pain in a relationship I say this prayer and it brings me back to the consciousness of the present moment, the only place a relationship can truly blossom.

Here's my Prayer which I've named, prayer for a co dependant woman in gest, it's my gift to you.

Prayer of a codependent woman

God I have faith, I trust your process with me and...(name of the person)

I hand over my fears and my insecurities and my need to possess love

I hand over my attachment to the thrills of his company

I handover my need to have control and guarantees on the future

I handover my jealousy of his freedom and his not needing me

I stand in my sovereignty, in my own synergy

I stand as the soul of this space right now and in my own greatness

I need not defend myself, I need not seek attention

I need not seek love, I experience my own self love

I need not seek validation, I experience my own beauty,

Knowing I am whole and complete just the way I am

Thank you God for hearing me

Thank you God because you always do

Amen

Share with us where in the world you are reading from and what lessons you are getting?

Go on share your view:
www.facebook.com/RelationshipsIntensive

CHAPTER FOUR

When Destiny Knocks You Answer

I'm coming up to 15 years old and loving life, It's been 3 years since we moved to Colombia. What I'd feared so uch has turned into what I love the most. I'm loving school, my friends, my motorbike rides and on Sundays I go to church. I help Mum out in her P before going out for a few hours in the evening with Daniel. I was very comfortable, dad was supporting me from the UK and I was a good kid that got involved in local community projects through a young leadership group, life was good.

And then one fateful day, the day that would change the course of my life forever, I had a visitor. He was an old friend of my dad's. I hadn't seen him in years, since I was a kid in the UK and he just came from nowhere, randomly showing up at our home behind the pharmacy in our small, remote town. We sat at our dining table for one of the longest conversations I had ever had until that point in my life. He said to me: "So, what's your plan? What are you doing here?" "What do you mean, what am I doing here? I said a bit confused by his opening question. My Mum's here and I'm with my Mum." "But" he says, "You have a British passport, you speak English. What plan do you have for life?" And I'm like, "Well, I guess I'll go to Uni, learn a couple of languages, I don't know, not given it much thought" And then he said, "Do you not think that the fact that you were born somewhere else, that you speak the language, do you not think that maybe it's got something to do with where your destiny lies? Do you not think that maybe you were born for bigger things?"

And so this became one of those moments where I knew Destiny was knocking, and when destiny knocks, you answer. He was the first 'angel' to cross my path, I don't know where this guy came from. He had never visited us before. I hadn't seen him since I was a kid. He just sat me down for about three hours, completely inspired me, my soul just knew that every word that came out of his mouth was just so true.

I was only 15 years old and within about a week I made a decision. I sat my Mum down, baring in mind I'm Mums' princess and best friend. I said, "Mami…'' took a deep breathe, "Madre, I think I need to go back to London." As I spoke, I felt it came from somewhere deep inside, deeper than me, it resonated so powerfully that she looked at me deep in the eyes and she said, in a sobered, paused manner; "Honey, that's a decision you need to make by yourself." Now imagine. Picture this. I'm 15 years old, I'm her only daughter, I often wonder where she got the courage and detachment to say that, but I know again, this came from somewhere deeper and bigger than ourselves, I know my Mum knew deep down that her little girl wasn't meant for her, although her human self regretted that choice many times after that, her higher self always knew her little girl was meant for the world. As scary a time that was in making that decision to leave everything I knew, I really believe that when you listen to your heart and take those types of leaps, as Paulo Coelho beautifully says in the Alchemist, the whole universe conspires to help you.

So there it was, three months later I stood at Heathrow Airport and suddenly this wave of fear ran all over me and I exclaimed, "Anna, What the f*ck did you just do!?" At that moment, I just looked up to the heavens, took a deep breath and said; "*God. I have no idea why I'm here, but PLEASE, just make me your instrument.*"

I had no idea what I was saying. I had no idea of the power of that prayer. I didn't know it at the time but the following ten years would become the making of the instrument. The making of me.

Although my dad lived in London with his wife and her two children from her first marriage, my slightly older step brother and sister, I couldn't face living with him, I loved him to bits but he could be quite jealous and controlling at times and I was just too grown up now. I was 15 going on 30 and my dad still wanted me to be his baby girl and I just wasn't going to have that.

So off I went to live with my uncle and his partner, who would become my auntie, a soul sister and later on to always be called my 'comadre'; mother to my first Goddaughter.

I would head out everyday after school to iron shirts at a beautiful riverside penthouse owned by a famous entrepreneur, it was my uncles'contract and I'd help out and get paid and that's how I began to grow my love for working for myself and for riverside living! I'd see my dad and the family every weekend but I never really felt home there, I was home with my uncle.

One day minding my own business, I received a

call from JC back in Colombia, he was always into the next business venture and this time he had an opportunity for me to support him and make big money. Well I liked the sound of that. He said he had a great contact in the mining of emeralds and that he was going to send me a sample so I could see what interest I might find in London for them. This sounded simple enough, so he did. I received a tiny little set of bears and on the phone he instructed me on how to dismantle them and in the bears hollow body I would find, buried in some plasticine, the tiniest and most beautifully cut green stones I'd ever seen. There were six of them. There's me in my innocence, thinking this was all very normal, I didn't realise the extent to which he had gone to camouflage them and therefore that perhaps this was illegal?! I mean I didn't know what I had in my hand. I didn't know the value of them. He instructed me. He said, "Why don't you go to a few jewelers and find out whether they're interested and see what you can get for them."

So, there's me in my school uniform somewhere near Tower Bridge, where I'd remembered there was a jewellers. I walked in with a big smile on my face, "Hello, darling. How can I help you?" Said the gentleman behind the counter. "Yeah, I was hoping you could." I said in my animated, and optimistic voice. I approached him and stretched my arm over the glass counter full of precious jewelry. I opened my hand and we both looked down at these beautifully cut, tiny green stones.

His eyes just lit up. I said, "Could I just check, would you have any interest in these? And roughly how much might they be worth?" Bless Me and my beautiful innocence. He looked at me with big eyes and seemed to be trying not to let his mouth open too wide, he then very calmly took one from my hand and put in under what looked like a posh microscope to check it. He stood still for a moment contemplating the stone and said "Honey, do you have more where this came from?" I smiled and exclaimed in pure innocence; "Yeah. Loads where that came from and I have plenty of access!" JC had explained that he had the best contact for ongoing supply, the guy worked inside the mine and had found a great funnel, whatever that meant! The kind gentleman went on; "Sweetheart, just these six alone, we're talking six or seven figures here." Now I didn't have a clue what that meant. I just stood there staring at him whilst I tried to imagine a number with that many figures in it. I was in my head still trying to figure it out when he interrupted me.

Then it was almost like an angel had descended

upon him and he looked at me with so much love and said, "But honey, you've got a choice to make here. In life you choose the route that serves your heart or you choose the route that serves your ego, if you choose to go down this path, it may not serve your heart and you seem to me like a pretty cool kid, like someone who can choose whether or not to do something. What choice are you going to make?" as this man spoke, I almost felt like I was touched by God or by angels, by something. As I listened to him, I was spaced out, I blinked slowly and I took the emeralds back from his extended hand and I very slowly began to retract my steps. Literally walking backwards, still looking at him. I couldn't give my back to him. I was shocked that this man and the opportunity he'd just let go of because something told him that this wasn't my destiny. I'm sure he was gutted afterwards.

I walked out of there not realizing at that moment that I'd just made one of the biggest choices of my life, Id chosen to follow my heart and that courage is always rewarded. I learnt later that I should follow my own dream, not anybody else's. I realized that it would have no integrity whatsoever. I realized that, that was not my destiny. I wasn't going to throw away my education or my training. In that moment, it didn't resonate with me. I was so grateful for that man, in that moment. About a year later when I flew back to Colombia, I took them back and I said, "Here you go. This is yours. This is nothing to do with me. I'm not interested." And in that moment I made the decision that it was never in my interest to do anything or to earn money in a way that I couldn't sleep with at night. In a way that wasn't aligned with me. I think that, that was a really important lesson. Especially, though I loved this man very much, it became very clear to me that I wasn't going to let a man's dreams get in the way of my own destiny. It was a real crossroads for me in that moment. Even though I was just 15 at the time.

That's when I made the solid choice, that no matter what happened in my life, the only thing I was going to stick to was my destiny, my journey, my thumb print, even though it would still be years until I'd come to learn what this was.

The Gifts in a nutshell:

- Life always gives you the opportunity to chose from a space of love or from a space of fear. And every choice you make, makes you.
- Your whole life can change in a day, a conversation, a choice or an instant.
- Following your heart is very likely to uproot you from what you know, from your comfort zone, your friends or your family. But great courage is eventually greatly rewarded.
- Learn to listen to your own heart, you have a unique journey and nobody else can live or understand it the way you can. Play your own instrument in the orchestra of life and leave each to their own.

Please come and share with us the lessons you are getting here, it could really make a difference Where in the world are you reading from? Connect with us today;

Go on share your view:
www.facebook.com/RelationshipsIntensive

CHAPTER FIVE

Vulnerable & Homeless: The Gift

This is a part of the story I blocked from my memory for the longest time because it had been wrapped in a lot of shame. I was 17 when I became pregnant, I was living with my auntie M or Tia, as I would call her in Spanish, she's my mums' sister and my Godmother through confirmation. She was one of the many places I called home during my teens. I shared a room with my Kucci, my cousin, although not my sister, she was my baby sis from the first moment I laid eyes on her. I was only 4 years old when she came to the UK, she was only 1 years old and the most adorable creature I had ever set my eyes on. I never forgot that first moment, she was smaller than me and had the biggest cheeks ever which I just couldn't resist so I grabbed exclaiming 'Hola Kucci Kucci!!' To which her first reaction was a very frustrated: 'me no Kucci, me Pola'. So Kucci we became to each other and soul sisters. From that moment on, we would have a bond that would last a lifetime. Tears come to me as I get present to my love for her and how tight we held onto each other through our mums' journeys battling with mental health.

We lived with uncle George, who was new to the family then, Tia had recently married and I found him super funny and cool from the first instant. Although misunderstood by most when he first joined the family, he came to show his value to all of us in good time becoming a strong male model and an oasis of comfort to me during times of hardship.

Bless my Tia, she was always trying to make everyone's life easier around her and in this case, taking me in, shortly after resettling back in the UK. She did this for me and for her sister, she knew I'd be safer with her, or so she planned. This was the fifth family home I had moved into since returning from Colombia two years before. I was 17 and had just started seeing my Tazmanian Devil, HP as I'd later come to refer to him. When I brought him home to introduce him to Tia, she loved him up instantly, making me feel even more welcome and loved. In those early days, any opinion held of my boyfriend or lover was directly correlated to their opinion of me. She'd let him stay over at the weekends as she preferred to keep me close to her and under wraps. So she'd let us have space for us to be together and she'd always remind me to make sure I was being safe. I'd smile shyly saying 'yes yes Tia, dont worry, Im on the pill. '

Omg, little did she know I was practicing unprotected sex. I was too ashamed to go to the doctors and ask for the pill. My non practicing, yet catholic inbuilt conditioning guilt kicked in. I just couldn't face a doctor to ask them for help. This was the first time fear would win its' battle over me and so within three months of dating, I became pregnant. It was only then I learnt he had two children back home from a previous relationship. I was terrified. I thought of my mum and my older brother G. How would I ever tell them?

The first person to know however was my Kucci, she was only 14 but was wise beyond her years. We had twin beds and everyday the first thing I would see was her beautiful face and olive skin as she slept, to me she looked like Eva Mendes, but she hated me telling her that. I was always an early riser so I would lay there lost in thought or meditation as I waited for her to wake up before we got ready for our daily trip to school. This time I was troubled however, with all sorts of emotions as I held onto my belly. As I put my fingers on my naval it had a separate beat and it would make my fingers jump.

As soon as she opened her eyes I ushered her excitedly towards me, she lept out of bed and sat next to mine. I took her soft hand and placed it over my belly button and looked at her in anticipation as her hand was pushed up and down by this strange beat. Her eyes widened, she looked up at me and gasped; 'What is that?' I smiled widely 'Oh My God' she shouted in a whisper, 'you're pregnant?!' I nodded, she hugged me and I said, 'No one knows; I'll let you know when I'm ready to tell'. If there was one thing I could count on Kucci for was her discretion and sensitivity. She never failed me.

I never plucked the courage to tell Tia, she figured it out. 'Honey, you're pregnant aren't you?' 'Why Tia?' I said tongue in cheek, not knowing what else to say. 'Sweetheart, I know what it's like to be so young trying to hide a pregnancy'. She sat me down and with tears in her eyes pleaded with me that I should have an abortion, that I could give myself a second chance. She told me I had a choice and that life didn't have to go this way for me right now. She was desperate for me to free myself from what she saw as something that would halt my studies and make my life so difficult. I completely understood where she was coming from and it made sense but I couldn't do that. As petrified as I was, there was a big part of me that felt I was finally going to be whole and complete. That this child would finally fill the void of emptiness that had become my faithful companion for the longest time.

I remember the first time I felt that feeling of inexplicable sadness, I was in my early teens in Colombia, I'd often just burst into tears in Daniel's arms. He never understood why I would often feel so sad and only find comfort in his arms. I was 13 the first time I ever experienced what I since came to recognise as depression. Whether it was behavioural conditioning from watching my mum all my life or a chemical imbalance, to this day I'll never know for sure, but what I do know is that my soul started to cry from that age. It was crying for something I didn't know. Daniel was an angel and patiently just held me in silence as we sat on the porch every evening, these episodes would sometimes last for periods of up to two weeks at a time. He just thought I was missing my dad, or dealing with changes in my family. The truth was, I never had a real reason. Or so I thought.

So here I was at 17 with the possibility of having a life that I could call mine, an extension of me, someone that would never leave me because I knew I'd become her best friend. Yes, I intuitively knew it was a girl. And I wasn't going to let her go for dear life.

So after my poor Tia tired of begging, she resigned herself and then went onto the next best thing, making sure I had a home for my new family and this is when I came to start realising who I was really about to have a baby with.

I remember his reaction when I told him he was about to be a dad: 'Oh my God, I'm not even 30 yet and I'm onto my 3rd child'. That was his reaction to my life changing news. He had two children under 3 by his previous partner back home in Colombia. He was 10 years older than me... yes he was. I was saddened by his response but I understood his concern and I let it go. He said nothing about us settling in or creating something together. And this is when Tia stepped in, bless her, she can be a bull when it comes to us. 'HP you guys can't carry on like this, Anna here and you somewhere else, you're going to need to create a home for yourselves' I waited expectantly but I never expected what was about to come out to come out of his mouth: 'I have a lot of responsibilities, I have a family to look out for you know' at this point the bull's nostrils flared, oh dear, this is never good. When this happens, you get out of Tia's way, she is kicking in the sand and you're waving red at her. 'Anna and this unborn child are now also your family and they are YOUR responsibility! 'She said in a powerfully raised voice. Well that came out very decent, I thought.

And sadly what I was thinking inside of me was 'Please Tia, don't make him do this' I honestly believed him. Errr? oh my God right? I know, I know, but this was me at 17, almost 18 and I really believed I wasn't worthy or loveable, that I didn't belong anywhere and that I wasn't good enough.

So that heated discussion led to HP finally agreeing that he should take me with him and create a home together for our child. My idea? Well he worked, so maybe he could rent us a small place somewhere, even if just a room so at least we could be together? Oh dear, this was my first lesson in lack of self love leads to lowering your standards which leads to very low expectations and therefore life results. I ended up living in a hostel that I wasn't supposed to be in, looking after a 3 year old stepson full time and sharing a bathroom and kitchen with another 5 families.

After the nightmares I lived through in that

hostel which I describe in the first chapter and after the loss of my child, I moved another two times until I was eventually housed by an association in North London with the support of an organisation which to this day I am grateful for and still remember the name off; the Kipper Project, an East London based project setup to support young people from troubled backgrounds, homelessness or fleeing abuse.

I was so incredibly grateful the day the support worker took me to my new flat and introduced me to my housing officer who would guide me with things like setting up with utility accounts, how to stay safe at home and even where to get furniture from. Yup, I didn't have a piece of furniture to my name. I was given vouchers that I could use to buy the basics which I did, I couldn't believe how blessed I was. That first night I slept on the cushions of a sofa that had been left behind on a corner of the living room. I had one of the usual fights with HP that day, these always seemed to happen at those most crucial life moments when I could've done with his help. But as usual, it was my family that were always there. My uncle Herman, love the bones of him. He has against all odds and chances, happened to be around every time I moved from the age of 15, I visualise him with a cape and tight pants, ok, maybe not the tight pants. I have moved over thirty times in my thirty-seven years of life.

That night as I lay alone on the floor in a corner of my new place I cried tears of gratitude, I couldn't believe that I had finally arrived at a place I could call mine. A very humble beginning, yet a place which would witness my growth for 16 years through much pain and joy and see me blossom and become.

So Hackney was the cradle of my career and of a fresh start in life, I had no idea the community I lived in until I started working with the local unemployed youth. I loved every moment of it, and although my participants walked into my rooms apprehensive, they always left with a smile and much love in their hearts. I felt every young hoodie in hackney knew me and it felt bizarrely cool and safe! Hackney was coincidently the borough I happened to be born in 24 years earlier.

I thought it was home, But I wasn't home yet. Hackney gave me my career, my first home, my confidence and colleagues that would become some of my best friends forever. Despite all of this however, my eyes were set on the beautiful Royal borough of Greenwich. From Hackney I'd travel to Greenwich everyday and for five years

I built a community of friends and family that would grow with me.

Greenwich was the borough that would gift me and my team the opportunity to grow discoverME through its' partnership with schools and children's centres, facilitating transformation in the lives of hundreds of families across South East London.

One of my life's greatest highlights was the day I realised I was able to choose how and where I would love to live. That's the day I chose to move to my dream home, a 3 bedroom house with a huge garden and parking for 3 cars. 'Why would you move into a 3 bedroom house by yourself Anna?' 'Because I love it' I would say. What can you say to that? When you make choices from the heart, you find you don't need to justify yourself and this is what I was beginning to savour for the first time in my life. For the first time I wanted to follow my heart and play to its' music. It was the best choice I ever made, I brought my mum over for an extended summer holiday and she rejoiced in our family gatherings, parties, gardening to her green heart's content and connecting with all my friends and network. They were incredible years, even if they were only to be a few.

From no home to dream home was a great achievement but the greatest achievement after that was growing as a person and detaching so much that I came to realise that what I needed was not in anything or anyone and all I wanted to do was to serve big and for that I needed to become lighter. The final chapter will tell you how I went from dream home to no defined home because home is where my heart is.

The Gifts in a Nutshell:

When we believe we are unworthy, unlovable and not good enough, we lower our standards, teach people to treat us accordingly and accept, in many cases the unacceptable. We teach people how to treat us, the man makes the woman and the woman makes the man. The mother makes the daughter and the daughter makes the mother and so on with all our relationships.

- Our limiting beliefs form part of our undercurrent, the behaviour we are unaware of which sabotage our relationships and cause attachments and suffering. These continue to exist but in awareness we can short circuit them and not be victim to our mechanisms.
- When someone questions your choices, if they come from your heart, you can answer with a very simple: 'Because I love it' What can they say to that?
- When we become whole and complete in who we are, we are in love with ourselves truly, we don't need to fill our lives with attachments, addictions whether in the form of people or material things or power symbols. We can actually free ourselves from a lot of baggage if we chose to let go.

Go on share your view:
www.facebook.com/RelationshipsIntensive

CHAPTER SIX

He's not your dad, I'm sorry

As a Masters student at the age of 23, I'm living with my mum and stepdad who I adore and are back in the UK. My mum and I have an amazing relationship. We're really good friends. However, my mum has always been emotionally codependent with me. She always suffered from depression. I remember, as a young kid, we used to have funny conversations, I used to say to her, "Mummy, I think sometimes I'm like your Mummy." And she'd go, "Yeah, I think you were probably in another life, you were my mummy." so I was very mature growing up.

So, I'm at University doing my Master's degree at this point and one normal afternoon as I'm halfway through writing my dissertation, she sits me down with a cup of tea and says; "Honey, what's the worst thing I could ever say to you?" I said, "Mum, that you're getting divorced for the third time!" she looks at me with a cheeky smile and says, "Noooo, Now why would you say that?" We giggle as she goes onto say with a more ominous voice, "Honey, there's something I need to tell you." I looked at her, I turned towards her and teary eyed she said to me, "Your dad is not your dad."

I'm looking at her and I am in absolute shock receiving this information. My first reaction was," Oh, my God. Is this what has been the cause of your mental health issues Mum?" "I've been carrying this secret since you were conceived" she said. 'absolutely nobody knows but an Irish priest from many years ago."

Instead of reacting with the questions of who's my dad and what happened? I just hugged her. I hugged her and I said, "Mama, free yourself. If I'm the reason that you have suffered from mental health and depression your whole life, I cry tears of joy. So is this it? Is this it?" She cried in my arms. She cried and she cried, "Forgive me, forgive me. I've held this secret for all my life. Not even Nando knows." Nando's my step dad.

I'm like, "Oh, my God, mami. You need to unburden yourself." So I wiped her tears. I was like, "Mama, it's okay. I'm here. You're here and that's all that matters'' And then it suddenly dawned on me that for the past half hour or so,

Id learnt dad wasn't my dad, but then WHO WAS?! 'Ok mum, so who's my dad?' I asked with the excitement of a girl about to meet her blind date. By this point I began to wonder and try guess in my own mind. My first guess; maybe my first stepdad, J's dad. But I didn't say anything. Then she went on to say; "Well, the only reason why I'm telling you this is because you recently met your sisters and your brother again. You knew each other as children and you bumped into each other again." I'm like, "Oh my God."

So, why did she choose to tell me this now after 23 years you may ask? So to answer this, let's rewind about six months.

I was in a restaurant with my boyfriend and a lovely lady came up to me and says, "Anna. Oh my God. Are you G's little sister?" I'm like, "Yes, who are you?" And she goes, "Do you remember me? I'm Amparito, mum to Alex & the twins? Remember? Look!" And she pointed at them and they waved, "Oh my God." I exclaimed. And it felt so amazing to meet them again after so many years because we were childhood friends.

And since that moment, we were inseparable, the following weekend I brought them home to my mum's, mum and Amparito had been best of friends back then too. Us kids were all kind of similar ages and we all had partners, there were six couples in total and we used to go out every weekend. It was just wonderful. There was such a great energy between all of us.

But one fateful night, my mum comes across a documentary about people who fall in love with their brothers and sisters not knowing that they were related and the tragedy that comes with it. And in that moment my mum decides, oh my God. What if Anna falls in love with Alex? This is what gives her the courage to come out into the open. Otherwise my mum may probably never have told me.

So she says to me, "Your dad is BG." I know at this point from the twins, that he lives in the States, he divorced from Amparito many years ago and has remarried.

I'm like, "What?" And nothing can ever describe the feeling of excitement, that moment of a-ha! that makes so much sense and oh my God, what am I going to tell my dad? All in one. Like it's such an encounter of emotions. But my first priority was just hugging her and saying, "Mum, I need you to let this go now. I am fine. Look at me. I am fine. Can you see I'm fine?" "Yes."

"Okay, good. Can you let this one go?" "Yes."
"Mum, you were a kid. You were 21 years old."

And she went on to tell me the whole story.
Apparently he was a bit of a Casanova and he
gave her what my dad wasn't giving her at the
time. She was being neglected and BG gave her
so much love and passion she said: "I so wanted
a child like Alex. I wanted a child like that. And
I made you with so much love." I'm like; "Mum!
too much information!" "I made you. Please
know that I sought for you. You were so
wanted.'' she went on. 'And then you came out."
'And I have been mummy's little princess ever
since' I finished her sentence. 'Yes, she smiled'.

Now, in that moment, my mum swore that he
knew. "He knows. Oh, he knows. He knows."
"Please,'' she said,. She insisted that my
biological father knew. "can we just keep this
between us?" She pleaded. I agreed, as long as
she could finally be happy, but in that moment
she swore me to secrecy.

I said that was fine, my only concern was my
mum. I remember that night I went up to the
bathroom and I was looking at myself in the
mirror. For the first time I looked at myself and I
saw myself as someone completely different. So
many things became apparent. I realized why I

never felt I belonged to the Garcia clan. I was so different. My traits, my personality traits were so different. My values were so different.

But then I looked at myself in the mirror and I stopped, and then, suddenly, it hit me. Tears began to roll down my face, the lips that I always thought were my dad's, weren't. My hips, that were a topic of comical conversation among the family for their similarity with my Garcia aunties, were no more. It all hit me slowly... Gradually and then within a couple of weeks I started to break down. I started to have the most incredible thoughts. And then it started to kick in.

What began to kick in was, I guess a type of mourning. See, we grieve in different ways and I was grieving the loss of my father and I didn't realise. I didn't realise how much it meant to me to be a Garcia and I had identified myself as being daddy's little princess, even though we had been estranged for the past five years or so. When my mum first gave me the news I was like, I'm not too happy with my dad anyways. He's in Colombia, minding his own business. He doesn't care about much anyway." Blah, blah, blah. Then, it hit me. I couldn't call my dad on the phone anymore, I couldn't call my dad acting like everything was fine because I was lying just by omission. It was one of the most painful things. As much as I wanted to, I just couldn't lie to him so I stopped calling.

In the meantime, my relationship with my mum became tense for the first time ever. We began arguing over petty things which we'd never done before. One day, it just blew out of control for me, it just hit me and I just couldn't be in her space anymore. Suddenly I got present to the fact that I was lying to my dad, I was holding onto my mum's secret, and I was resenting her for having me hold onto that secret with my siblings who I was hanging out with and I couldn't tell them. Every time I was in front of those twins, my twin sisters, Paula & Anna we We're like triplets, I loved them to bits and we told each other everything, we were so close, Yet every time I was with them I was lying. The worse part was going to my brother Alex's wedding, it was heartbreaking to not be able to tell them how much Id come to love them even more after finding out we were blood. They are three of the most sincere, down to earth and kind people I've ever met. Them and their mum treated me like family and I always felt right at home with all of them.

My whole life had suddenly became a lie and I

couldn't do it anymore. So, eight months of all this became unbearable and I didn't know who to turn to, I had to call someone I had to tell someone. I was going crazy. So who did I call? I called my big brother G.

When I rang him to say I needed to talk, he knew it was something serious because I never called him. This would be my brother's second intervention. He is like, Sherlock Holmes' older brother, Mycroft. He's got my back but from a distance. We met up in a sunny pub garden near Milend in East London. It was the longest conversation I'd ever had with him. It was four hours long and I told him everything. He looked at me with teary eyes and he said, "You know, I'm just disappointed that I thought you were my only full sister." Of my mums four children we were the only ones to share the same surname and dad, or so we thought. None of us have the same mom and dad. He said, "I actually thought you were my only full sister." That was his biggest disappointment. He suddenly developed this big urgency to save me. I was in such distress. He said, "All right. You're coming with me. I don't care what Stacey says," (his wife,) "You're coming with me." So, that was the second time my brother saved my ass. I moved in with my brother and my sister in Law, she was an amazing support to me and we lived eight great months together although I still went into a deep depression. I was just graduated, jobless, kind of homeless and so lost.

Then we haven't even got to the toughest part of this story...telling my dad the truth. There was no way I could hold onto that secret anymore, it had to come out.

My sadness was not only mourning the loss of my dad but the realisation that mum had sworn me into secrecy and I resented her incredibly for that. She'd carried this weight all her life and it cause-d her so much pain but now I was sharing that pain and to top things off, I was bang in the middle of a huge identity crisis. I was looking at myself every day and I'm like God, who am I? Who am I? Oh my God. And I had to hide it from my sisters. I didn't want to spend time with them anymore because I was lying to everybody. I couldn't call my dad because I was lying to him.

So, finally after a significant amount of time with my brother, I think, I don't know, two, three months. I was unemployed, looking for work. I was not having any success. I turned around to him and I said, "I can't do this anymore. I have to go to Colombia. I have to go and tell my dad." He said, "Are you sure that's what you want to do?" I said, "I need to know the truth. I need to know that he knows. Then he can decide whether he wants to still be my dad or not." He said, "Fine. I'm going to pay for your ticket." "you're going to go out there, take your time, and tell my dad. But here's one thing I want you to know, if my dad rejects you, he doesn't lose one child. He loses two." And boom; his words brought shivers down my spine. My hero in action again; he brought me to tears, I felt so protected by him and so loved, and my brother had never really expressed himself in that way at all. But that moment I felt loved, incredibly loved, and I also felt a lot of pressure.

Doing the right thing is often the hardest thing. And by the right thing I mean following your heart's courage despite all fear and what may come as a result.

The Gifts in a Nutshell

- It's in moments of such raw pain that real love can be seen within ourselves because we are present to the moment and not in our ego minds.
- Life will eventually give us what we ask for, be mindful what you ask for and how you ask for it. In seeking my brothers love, life brought it to me through great pain. Today I pray to experience real love without the drama!
- Suffering comes from resisting the present moment for what it is. It was my identification with who I thought I was and wanted to be, "a Garcia" that led to so much pain.
- Does it matter what surname we carry or whose genes we carry when we are fulfilling on our mission? What if every single part of your story has been unfolding exactly as it should? Consider that it is and that every part of your physical and genetic makeup has been designed with the intention of fulfilling

your very own unique destiny.

What are you seeing for yourself?

How does this serve you?

Please do Share with us, where in the world you are reading from and what lessons you are getting?

Don't be shy; Go on share your view: www.facebook.com/RelationshipsIntensive

CHAPTER SEVEN

Conversation I'd Never Wish on You

I landed in Colombia, rocked up to my dad's restaurant. He had a beautiful restaurant there. My dad didn't even recognize me. I came up to the counter and I said, "Good afternoon, sir. How are you doing?" He goes, "Yes, ma'am. How can I help you?" I looked at him and I smiled and he said, "Oh my God. This is my daughter. Everyone, this is my daughter. This is my daughter.' He waved his arms around to get everyone's attention like a little kid, so adorable. And just what I needed to add to the guilt. 'Oh dear' I thought to myself, seeing the heart that I was soon to break. He got all excited. "My baby girl. My baby girl." Oh my God, my heart sank as I thought to myself, dad, you have no idea that I'm not your baby girl.

They lived across the road, my stepmum Consuelito and him. I hadn't seen her since I was in my teens; she welcomed me in: "My God.

What an amazing surprise." She smiled. " Come through. Let's set you up. Are you coming to stay with us? Fantastic." She was so welcoming and kind as always.

I stayed there for six weeks. It took me four weeks, FOUR weeks to pluck up the courage to have the conversation with my dad.

At the time, laser eye treatment was very much the trend in Colombia. Many stars from around the world would come to this particular clinic to get their eyes done because they were very good. So one day my dad surprises me and says, "Come on. We're going into town. I'm going to take you somewhere." We're suddenly walking into this clinic. Beautiful clinic. Next thing, he's booking an appointment for eye laser treatment. He knew I was going increasingly short sighted but I thought he was booking for himself. And then, suddenly I learned that it was for me. I panicked. And not because of the surgery; " oh my God. No, no, no." I'm thinking in my head; "my dad's making this grand gesture and he doesn't even know I'm not his daughter. Oh my God. And how do I say this to him. Oh my God.''

I had no choice, how could I refuse my dad's gift? So a few days later we were back for the actual surgery. After it was over, the nurse guided me to sit in a separate room where she was about to take off my eye patches, my dad was relieved to see me and comforts me with his warm voice welcoming me back. The nurse begins to take off the patches and I manage to see my dad with his expectant face. So much joy and happiness as he's looking at me. I couldn't help it and I started crying. The nurse put her arm over and exclaimed straight away "You can't cry young lady. You can't cry. You could ruin the surgery." Neither of them could understand why I was crying. I was guilt ridden. My dad had no idea he had just spent all this money on someone who wasn't his daughter, I felt like an imposter. I panicked inside 'What do I do?' I forced myself to calm down as he drove me home with the patches back on my eyes where I went on to sleep for a whole 24 hours.

For days I hadn't slept. I'd stay up whole nights trying to figure out how I could become my dad's daughter again. Nothing had changed, yet everything had changed for me with this. It was so excruciatingly painful. In my fantasies about how I could become my dad's daughter, I'd explore the wildest ideas on how I could do that. Could I get my mum and my dad together again? Maybe I could have a blood transfusion? No, that wouldn't work. I was desperate to belong, to be his again. How could I be my dad's daughter?

I was mourning the loss of my father, there's truth in what they say that you never know what you have until you lose it. I was grieving. I was going crazy, until finally one afternoon I couldn't take it anymore; the pain of the lie far exceeded my fear of rejection. "Papi, I need to talk to you." "Yeah, sure, hon. Talk to me." He said. "No, let's go for a drive." I said with a nervous sigh. Dad being dad, always wanting to make me happy responded with an enthusiastic: "Yeah. Sure. Come on then let's go". We started driving out of town. driving across the green plains of the stunning Coffee region, until we came to a stretch of beautiful restaurants on the side of the road. "How about this one?" he said pointing to one of many, "No, no, dad. Carry on."After another five minutes, "How about this one?" he said, "No, no, dad." not that one either. Dad looked confused at how fussy I was being, very unlike me. But the fact was no place felt right for what I was about to do. Nothing was.

Until finally we came across a place called 'La Vaca', the Cow. "Yes, this one will do'' I said almost under my breath. "This one will do." The pain was just unbearable. We walked in, it was a vast ice cream parlour with extensive gardens at the back and in its surroundings where lots of children played. I walked straight through the restaurant as if possessed and sat at the very end where the floor stepped onto the grass. I sat right there and dad just joined me, by this point seeming a bit worried about what was going on. I was so absent I didn't even sit down on a table and chairs like everyone else. I just sat on the floor with feet on the grass, facing the gardens where the children played. And we just sat there.

Finally he interrupted the silence, he looked at me and said: "Honey, what is it?" I said, "Pa, please forgive me, there is no way I could ever tell you... There's no way I could possibly put this ... I was sweating and shaking. " I'm just going to have to say it." I took a deep breath: "Papi, you're not my dad." ''I'm really sorry''.

My dad looked at me and his whole face just dropped, my heart sank. It was like the world stopped in that moment., "What? Did your mum get upset with you and she's been telling you lies?" He said in a desperate attempt for this not to be true. "Dad, come on. My mum's not that kind of person and you know that." I said.

"Okay, so is it Efrain, referring to J's dad" my first stepdad. "No, dad." I said softly, with pain in my eyes and my heart breaking as I saw my alpha male dad clinging onto his pride as he began a desperate guessing quest.

But his second guess was right. 'Is it BG?' I looked down at the floor feeling guilty as charged and then I looked into his eyes "Dad, I'm so sorry. I'm so sorry." He looked at me and I could see in his face, that his heart was breaking.

But as quickly as I saw pain, I saw his resolve and his protective instinct hijacked any heartbreak . He paused, looked at me with grace, smiled, and as he held back tears he went on to say words that would live with me forever. "Honey, you know what..? This information comes in one ear and out of the other. You have always been my baby and you will always be my baby."

And in that moment my dad wiped the board clean off anything I had ever held against him through my childhood. In that moment, my dad, for me, became an angel and I got my dad back. I never appreciated my dad as much as when I learned he wasn't my biological father. I held him, we hugged and he said to me, "Honey, I just want you to be happy. Nothing has changed."

Can you imagine that kind of man that my dad

showed himself to be in that moment? To me, he became my hero in that moment. He became my hero again. I was daddy's little girl again and he became my hero. For me it was like a reset button. He's just incredible.

Before I left to see my dad in Colombia, I called my mum, it had been about three months, since she'd told me. my mom was suffering at home crying her eyes out. She'd gone into a deep depression because I'd left. For the first time in my life I just couldn't put my mum's emotions before my own. I had to handle my own crisis. My step dad, at one point, he's so compassionate and patient all his life with mum and all of us. He texted me saying 'you're mum is suffering. I don't know what happened between you girls, but please, I beg you, sort it out with your mother.' I was devastated; and so angry that she hadn't told him. I knew he wasn't judging me, but I could imagine he was deep down. I didn't even text back. I just texted my mum 'please tell him. Please do it for your sake.'

When I was ready to leave for Colombia, I gave my mum a call. I said; "Mum, I'm so sorry, but I'm not committed to carrying what you have always carried, its just not my weight to carry and neither should you. It's not necessary. I don't do this to go against you. I'm doing this for me. I need to go and tell my father and I need everybody to know what is going on. At least those who are affected by this." It felt disheartening that I had to take the lead in all this. But I'd learned to accept and love my mum for who she was and who she wasn't. I came to understand today that she didn't have the emotional equipment, communication skill or confidence to face something like that, so she had to hide. So, I said to her, "Mum, I'm going to go and tell my dad and I'm going to ask you to have a conversation with Amparito". Amparito was my siblings' mum and also her good friend from when they were young.

My mum agreed and just two days before I was due to travel she made the dreaded call. How do you call your best friend and confess to her that you had an affair with their husband twenty plus years ago? But she did, for me: "I'm so sorry, but Anna is BG's daughter. I'm just so sorry. "I really hope you can find it in your heart to forgive me. I was young and I was stupid. I really just pray that you never hate my daughter. I know how much you love her."

Amparito in that moment, responded to her gracefully; "I thank you for telling me. I will never hate your daughter because I love her like my own. It doesn't come as a surprise, my mother always suspected it but I was always in denial. Regarding our friendship however, I'm sorry but I can never be your friend again, I trust you'll understand." And that was a choice that she made and as sad as that reality was to see a lifelong friendship die in an instant, I can completely understand. She's one of the most graceful women that I know, but it was too much pain to bear. And that was that.

That night Amparito called a family gathering with her three children: 'All right, kids, we need to talk'. On the other side of town I was packing, getting ready for my biggest conversation ever. She sat them down and she told them the news. Everyone has given me their own account of this moment, but it suffices to say for now that they each had a different response. I'm very close to them today, and I'm blessed to have them. The twins were delighted, "Oh my God. I knew it. I knew it. I always knew. I knew she was our sister." said one of the twins,

Whilst our brother took a more reserved approach. He's one year older than the twins. And my mum's godson. Being very protective of his mother, his response was a lot more conservative and centred around his mum. "Mum, how are you?" He said concerned about how this may be impacting her whilst The girls were jumping for joy exclaiming; "See. We were right. We always used to say we had a sister in London." Although born in London, contrary to me, they grew up in Colombia for most of their younger years. They went on in their excitement: "We always used to say this and look, it came true. It came true."

Next thing, in their excitement they just wanted to connect with me and celebrate their new found sister, welcoming me into the family. They're desperate to meet their sister because as much as we'd been hanging out for the last eight months or a year, they were desperate to meet with me as their sister.

We were in very different spaces; they were in a space of, oh my God, this is amazing whilst for now I was mourning the loss of my dad and my identity.

I just couldn't respond to their enthusiasm because for me, I needed to grieve the process of my dad before I could ever engage.

They kept ringing my phone and I wouldn't answer, Id stare at the flashing screen crying my eyes out knowing they just had so much for me and just wanted to reassure me.

I eventually plucked up the courage to text back:

"I thank you. I thank you for your response. I thank you. Please just give me some time."

Amparito was amazing as well and she made her love for me very clear and also reminded me that is wasn't my fault and she was always going to be there for me. I love her to bits and for me she's another mum. I've been blessed with quite a few of them.

The Gifts in a Nutshell:

- It doesn't matter how much fear you have, courage is always rewarded and the gift will emerge sooner or later if we are patient.
- When we speak our truth from a space of love and are prepared to take on whatever it brings, we access true power in our communication.
- Real love is thicker than blood. Does it really matter whether you are genetically connected when at a soul level, the connection is undeniable?
- It's not always guaranteed that you'll get the ending you wish for but sooner or later you learn it was the best ending within the grander scheme of things.
- Mourning doesn't just happen with death, we can mourn the loss of people even when they haven't died. But when suddenly they don't play a role in your life or their role transitions, it is normal and it is ok to allow yourself to mourn.

What are you finding for yourself?

*We'd love to hear from you .Please do share
with us. Tell us where in the world you are
reading from and what lessons you are getting?*

*Go on share your view:
www.facebook.com/RelationshipsIntensive*

CHAPTER EIGHT

A Facilitator is born

I was 24 years old, going through an identity crisis, unemployed, desperately trying not to become yet another unemployed graduate statistic. It had been a year since learning about my paternity. And my brother G had taken me in, he'd saved my ass yet again. Graduated from a Master's Degree in occupational Psychology was making me 'overqualified' for many jobs but inexperienced for a consultancy role in occupational psychology, which was the next, supposedly natural step to take. I'd made it my job to look for work but it became tougher each day; with every rejection, my self-esteem lowered and my confidence got knocked. As my limiting beliefs got triggered it exacerbated the pain of loss I was already experiencing and it was very quickly that this led me into a rut of depression. I felt I wasn't good enough, that I didn't belong, that I was powerlessness and I began to isolate myself more and more over the coming months. I isolated myself from family and friends in shame and even from my brother and sister in law who I lived with. I'd very often hide away in my room like a mouse as soon as they arrived home from work. It was such a vicious circle because not connecting caused pain but the shame of the situation I was in caused me to want to do nothing else.

My brother and I had never been able to connect the way maybe many siblings do, the age gap had never helped and our separation at a young age meant we drifted apart even more. My sister in law always used to say that we were just too proud. She was right. We both struggled to connect but neither of us really made an attempt to. But this time life was forcing us to live under the same roof, giving us the first opportunity to connect through my vulnerability.

One evening as I hid in my dark bedroom lit up only by a small lamp in a corner I was wallowing in my sorrow listening to old hispanic ballads, this is what I had learnt to do through my upbringing which seemed like a separate world to that of G's. My world seemed to have been led by emotions and drama whilst my brother somehow had kept himself immune to it all, it seemed. There I was lying on my bed having one of my silent yet heartfelt, soul wrenching cries, when I heard a soft knock at the door. My brother came in, 'You alright sis?' he asked gently. I nodded looking down feeling embarrassed to be a burden. 'I feel so much pain' I said. 'Oh darling and this music doesn't help love' he said. I knew he was right, but in that moment I was savouring the pain and this music helped me. Not knowing what else to do or say, he left.

I knew I was in a rut, I didn't know how on earth I was going to get a job and it was here that I had my second moment of massive surrender to God.

The following morning I was sat in front of the computer. When I realised I was probably never going to be given the opportunity to train as an occupational psychologist consultant for lack of experience, this realisation hurt because I'd spent many hard nights studying towards a Masters degree I could do nothing with. It was that moment that I realised the source of my suffering. I was attached to working in that field because of the time and money invested in the qualification. I sat there and suddenly thought, what if that's not the plan? What if God doesn't need me to be that but needs me elsewhere? And it that moment I let go. I said God, I hand myself to you, may it be your will, I put my destiny in your hands now, I'm going to get out of the way and you show me.

Now when suffering leads us to these moments I REALLY believe in the power of those prayers. But also in the importance of following the heart as God begins to speak to you through it, and for that you need such courage and discernment.

'God I remove myself, I get myself out of the way and I have faith that you will show me the way. I will stay open, listen for the signs and have the courage to trust and action them. God I surrender to you. Thank you for hearing me, Thank you God because you always hear me'

Ahhh, that felt so good. Why carry all this weight when I can hand it over. I remembered that I am like a chess piece on the board of life and God moves the pieces. There's a path set from beginning to end which I came here to fulfil, I can either struggle it alone or let God/life/universe/ source/ heart, guide me.

In that moment, my energy shifted, I knew little about vibration and energy then, but I can tell you now that I went from fear into faith, into love and gratitude. In that lightness, one, I saw my life circumstance as it was, a life circumstance, not who I was. And I felt free from suffering.

To this day I know this moment to be testament

to the power of faith and shifting one's energy. Within the hour a uni friend called me. She'd been going through a tricky time finding work too but has resolved to seeking help.

"Why don't you go and find help from the job centre?" She said all animated. "Me? Go to the job centre? What and sign on?'' "Yes she exclaimed! You can get support in finding work and ease some of the financial pressure so you can focus on finding work.'' Gosh, my first reaction was to reject the idea and then I remembered the conversation I'd just had moments before with my creator. I never forget that phone conversation. She'd never called me before that day...nor did she ever call again.

I learnt that day that life speaks to us through people, events and whatever means he can find to do so. I mean, if it were your child, wouldn't you? I learnt there and then that all I needed to do was keep my heart open and willing to say yes to life. And this meant shedding some ego. Infact I've come to realise since then that every major breakthrough or growth, like a ladder move on snakes and ladders, is preceded by substantial ego shedding. And I now understand why...Because we need to be light to travel upwards.

So I swallowed my pride, faced my fear of being judged, took a deep breathe and walked into the jobcentre. I was seen to quickly and led to a desk where a young man greeted me. I handed him my CV and he took down my details. He was cool and kind, he was a representative of Working Links, one of the job centres' main providers at the time. When he was done with all the questions and data input, he looked at me almost apologetically, I thought he was about to say he couldn't help me: "Anna, I'm sorry, I can see you're very educated, but because you are still 24, I'm gonna have to put you on a course."

The fit4work programme was a two week confidence building and employability programme aimed at 18 to 24 year olds. To his surprise though, I almost leapt off my seat with excitement: "Yes, that sounds perfect! Please give me something to do. Give me some sort of structure, someone to help me.'' I exclaimed. I was so relieved that finally I wasn't going to have to do this alone and I'd be given some structure and something to go to and be a part of. I'd been missing this hugely.

Within a few days I was set to walk into the Working links offices at the Paragon building in Mare street, Hackney. This day would change my life forever and I would turn one of the biggest corners of my career, my very first one.

As I walked right through the middle of these modern open planned offices, I noticed the vibe was very different. Workers sat at their desks, seeing to clients with open body language and connection, they were smartly dressed but had a cool energy about them, they were relaxed and energised in their approach.

As I reached the medium sized, glass, training room at the end of the floor, where I had been directed to, I caught the wondering eyes of the worker sat on the last desk to my right. He smiled warmly and greeted me from his seat. I smiled back in appreciation of his warm reception and walked into the room. Here I was greeted by a really casual and kind trainer who welcomed me in and invited me to take a seat. I sat in the middle of a semi circle facing the trainer and a flipchart. The glass wall meant that everyone could see from the outside including the gentleman sat on the last desk.

As the trainer began to introduce himself and the programme I quickly noticed how much he enjoyed his work and I asked myself, 'are you allowed to enjoy your work that much?' up until that point Id only ever cleaned offices in the corporate world and most of them had looked like really tense and serious environments. And I honestly thought that work would have to look that way and that I would have to adapt to that to fit in. This trainer was so inspiring, he was fun and really connected to us. He made me feel right at home and very quickly I felt comfortable enough to volunteer to stand up and speak up when he asked us. I played full out and thoroughly enjoyed that day. I connected with other young people and felt I belonged somewhere for the first time in a long time. I felt good.

Half way through that week we were right in the middle of doing some group presentations when the man from the last desk stepped quietly into the room with a big smile and coyishly waiving at us all. As soon as the trainer finished his last sentence, he went on to introduce our guest. His name was Femi and he managed the training team. He'd come in to observe the trainer but I later found out more.

That afternoon when we were all saying goodbye, Femi came up to me and asked if he could have a word. 'Sure' I said, following him to his desk. I sat down and he had the biggest, friendliest smile I'd ever seen

"What the heck are you doing here?" He said. " I've been looking at your CV and I don't understand why you are here" "I don't know." I said sadly and I started crying. "I don't know". Femi put his arms around my shoulders, and reassured me that everything was going to be ok.

From that moment onwards, he took me under his wing. He became my first mentor and set me on the life changing path of finding out what I'd come here to do. I was never looking to become a facilitator, it found me. Femi sat me down with and introduced me to Daniel, his line manager. Daniel was just as kind and eager to help. I couldn't believe people at work could be so loving and kind and want to support me the way they did. And this they did. They quickly identified what my skills were and invited me to start up as a volunteer. Because of my background in Occupational Psychology, I was able to apply some measuring tools they needed at the time to evaluate the effectiveness of the fit4work programme and they loved it. And as a result of that, after a few months, they invited me to apply for a job as a trainer.

I was in shock, thrilled but petrified.

They were prepared to train me up as a trainer

on fit4work, the same programme I'd been put on which I'd loved. This was incredible. But also, this was the same mandatory programme that for many 18 to 24 year olds from Hackney felt like a total waste of time and inconvenience and so they met the programme with huge resistance and often quite aggressive in their resistance.

'So you're inviting me to stand in front of thirty, 18 to 24 year olds from Hackney who don't want to be there. You're kidding me, right?'

Nope, they weren't kidding and in fact they felt I'd be perfect for the job. So here I am suddenly on the other side of that prayer to God. ... *'I will stay open, listen for the signs and have the courage to trust and action them.'* So I did.

It was the most scary experience ever. So there I was on my first day stood in front of thirty-five kids. Some with their jeans halfway down their butts, their caps covering their eyes, and in some cases, their nostrils flared open in overt aggression! They're looking at me going: "Yo, yo so what you gonna teach me like- FAM!." I was so like "Oh, my goodness, help me." I wasn't up to date with their lingo, attitude or dress sense!

These were to become three of the most incredible, growth years of my training. I lived in Hackney, but I had no idea what was going on in Hackney. Half these kids were driving around in BMW's, they were dealing. The other half were incredibly talented and just needed a little guidance.

They didn't want to be a number. Femi was incredibly gifted in connecting with these kids and I learnt very quickly from him that they won't care what you have to say until they know you care. That's when I learnt they just needed to be loved. I learned to really love people without judgment. I learnt to see past their anger or current circumstance and see their greatness even when they couldn't. I learnt to be firm, provide structure and often tough love but it was always love. They'd start the programme being guarded and defensive but by the end of the first day, they'd brought down their walls and would be high-fiving me on their way out, saying: "Yo! see you tomorrow Miss." It was awe inspiring and often even funny to see bad boys go soft when they were met with love. When their ego was disarmed they were left present to love, appreciation and gratitude.

Through these types of transformation these kids

would go back into work quicker and sustain because their self love had grown. As a result my self love and confidence grew and this impacted my ability to serve.

I very quickly grew within the organisation, and began training trainers, and supporting other branches up and down the country to develop their training teams. That's when the facilitator was born, I did not go looking for it, I surrendered and the journey found me. I felt at home.

I loved witnessing human beings blossom, who had perhaps given up hope on themselves like I almost had for a brief moment. Just helping them restore their faith, see who they really were and as a result get back into work or education was life changing for me. I felt alive, on purpose and in flow with life again. I found life long friendships in my fellow trainers, Arzu, Ndidi, Grace and Libby who have played a crucial role in my growth by being there for me during my greatest and toughest times. And in Femi & Daniel, my first mentors who to this day I am also blessed to call dear friends. Life changed completely and I left my brother and sister in Law with much gratitude and moved into my own home again.

I enjoyed three years of solid training at

Working links, it was fun and it was tough at times. I grew as a person, a woman and as a facilitator. The mourning days were over and I reconnected with my mum and my family and friends. I felt good. I was enjoying all the choices that came from a decent earning, like salsa classes, going to the gym, decorating my flat, travelling with my girlfriends, going on holidays and most importantly, my self expression through my work and all the self love and confidence that I could gain from that.

Through the cultural diversity in the company, I was introduced to London's multicultural tapestry. Up until this point in my life, I had only ever experienced the Colombian way. I now had the choice to say yes to every opportunity to explore that came my way. The company gifted us monthly trips to the theatre, to musicals and through the cultural diversity of the team, I learnt to dance the electric slide and fell in love with Jollof rice!

My horizons were expanding and I was hungry for growth, much more growth. This had become my home, my family and I was so grateful. Id overcome my fears, I'd overcome homelessness and unemployment, I'd found my talent and developed my skills. Then… I began to feel that feeling again.. The feeling I had when I was 15 and I just knew I had to leave the comfort of home. Ahhh, why? If everything was so perfect? But that's what was wrong, it was comfortable, I realised I had come to the end of my growth journey here.

I prayed again. *'God, I have an urge in me to grow beyond what I have come to know as my comfort zone. Show me where you want me to go next'*. As expected many changes began to emerge.

One of them was my fairy God mother, Libby. She'd joined our training team a few years after me and we grew into unlikely friends very quickly. Libby was of a creative background and had such a calming presence, she was unassumingly elegant and graceful. The first time we spoke was for hours and that's when she introduced me into the magical world of personal development. Many answers came wrapped up in Libby's' words of wisdom and her invitations to evening talks in central london would change my life forever once again. Inspired by talks by Neal Donald Walsh and Don Miguel Ruiz, I got present to my soul beginning to call at me again saying there was something else that I needed to do. Being one who had learnt to listen, I did.

The first shift was finally ending my relationship with my boyfriend of five years, to be truthful, by year three I was exiting but hadn't had the heart, courage or self belief to do so. He'd been a huge support during my uni days and with dealing with my paternity crisis but the more I found myself, the further away from him I grew. Our values were very different but I was never to know that until I got clear on what mine were. I also had an ongoing fear that I may never find someone as kind or understanding as him.

But with my heart screaming out at me to honour my calling I had to leave. I now know that on our bus of life, people will come on and off at the most divine times, our problem is when we refuse to let them off and we stand in the doorway, in the meantime, stopping the perfect person or people from hopping on. Some people are meant to stay for the whole journey, others will hop on and off and others will hop off forever. But when we trust and let people go when we know we should, we then allow the best ones to come on board.

It took me a while and it was very painful, but eventually I let him go. And for three months I dived into yoga, gym, musicals and Salsa.

Something big was about to happen, I could feel it and I was ready.

The Gifts in a Nutshell:

- Trust the process; have faith that everything is unfolding as it should. This allows a clear space for life to happen.
- Learn to Listen to the signs and then have the courage to act on them.
- Become an observer of your limiting beliefs and know that they are not who you are. It's easy to have one belief trigger another and then another and suddenly feel really low and disempowered. For example "I'm not good enough", I don't belong, Im powerless, and the list goes on.
- When fear takes over, we attract more fear based events, when we shift our focus and our energy however into a love and gratitude vibration, life is able to flow with ease again and synchronicity becomes common.
- When we step through fear and say yes to life, life then takes huge leaps towards us. Shifting your mindset from Life is happening to me, or worst still against me, to life is happening for me and with me, your world changes.
- Life is waiting for you to show up because

everyday that you are not, there is a group of souls that have been assigned to you that are not being reached at by you. Imagine, how many people's' destinies are dependant on you stepping into yours? Fear keeps it all about you. Love reminds you it's not about you

---

Please do share with others what you are getting from the book so far. Tell us where in the world you are reading from and what lessons you are getting?

*Be in with a chance to win a **VIP** place at one of our Relationships Intensive Event.*

Go on share your view:
www.facebook.com/RelationshipsIntensive

CHAPTER NINE

Meeting my Soulmate & Letting him Go

It was salsa that brought me to him, I'd seen him at work but never paid any attention. P worked in another department and like me, he had joined a group that were going salsa once a week after work. One night as I was leaving he asked if I would give him a lift, I didn't realise he lived only ten mins away from me, 'sure' I said with a smile, sweaty and still out of breath from the awesome salsa session we'd just had. We got talking, P, striked me as a kind, chilled out and calm guy, he was attentive. As I drove up by his door he said 'I really like you Anna' I was totally not expecting that. I blushed. Soon after he invited me out on a date. This was my first date ever. I'd actually never been on an official date. Let alone with someone who wasn't colombian and in this case black!

I'd never imagined myself going out with a black man. P was born in the UK with Caribbean parents. He was eleven years older than me and barely looked older than me. He was such a breathe of fresh air, he was chilled yet grounded, wise and goofy, he was so funny yet tactful.

He was beautiful. It quickly became apparent that we were meant to be together and so we did. Whenever I was in his arms I felt at home, it was easy and it was peaceful. I worried because he had a son. I was 25 by this point but with so many unresolved issues, including childhood issues that were triggered by P's relationship to his son.

Growing up I always felt like I never belonged within the family. I always felt, as a stepchild I always felt like, I was the odd one out. It never sat well with me to be somebody's stepmother. It just never sat well with me. So from the beginning I always told him, "It's just probably not going to work, it's probably not going to work, it's going to be really difficult." Despite my concerns, we went on to have three of the most magical years together.

And it was P who cheered me on and supported me to take the plunge of finally leaving work. I knew I had to go at it alone, I knew I had to set up my own thing. I didn't know what I was going to do, but I knew I had to follow my heart. I knew I had to set up my own company.

But before I did, P also knew how much I had missed out on in my earlier years due to hardship and taking on so much responsibility. He'd travelled quite extensively whereas this was something I longed for. My soul was yearning to travel and this was a big missing piece for me. So not only did he encourage me dare greatly with my career but he encouraged me to finally fulfil on my dream of travelling. And so off I went with his blessing to travel through Colombia and Peru for three months. In Peru I met with my girls Arzu and Ndidi and we had a once in a lifetime trip through the ruins of Machu Pichu, sailing on lake Titicaca and a life-changing visit to Cusco. We were not the same women by the end of that trip. We got to know ourselves deeply and our friendship grew stronger.

Halfway though my trip, back in Colombia, P came out to visit me, I remember feeling like a little kid as I anticipated his arrival at the airport. It was wonderful to introduce him to the whole family and it was hard for everyone, including my dad to not fall in love with him.

Consuelito loaned us her brand new car and we set off on an unforgettable road trip through the

North West region towards the coast. Wherever we went groups of kids would come up to P and ask him if he was a famous american basketball player. He would chuckle and play. P was playful and so light in his nature, he gradually taught me the art of removing drama from my life and a lot of the pain that hid in my heart.

We arrived in Cartagena, a beautiful, colonial city on the coast of Colombia, home to some of the most beautiful architecture and boat trips to nearby islands. We boarded a tourist speed boat to an island two hours of the shore of Cartagena. As we arrived, they served us fresh fish for lunch. We then went for a walk and discovered some hammocks looking out to the sea, we were literally in paradise. We lay on this perfectly handcrafted hammock for two and as he held me in his arms I realised how blessed I was. Knowing that soon he would head back home for me to continue on my journey, it was then that it just felt like the perfect moment to ask him to marry me. And as I did, he asked me straight back, 'Will you marry me?' And straight away it was a yes from both of us. It was such a beautiful moment. We'd spoken many times about getting married before then but it was just a perfect moment. And so there it was, we were engaged.

No sooner had we'd agreed to engage and I'd head back to our home in the UK, that my soul would begin to speak to me again. It was the same familiar feeling. I dreaded it when it showed up because it always made me abandon my plans. I began to rationalise to justify the feeling that this wasn't it. He wanted children. He wanted to have a child before he was 40 and that was soon. That was very soon. He wanted to marry very soon, and he wanted to do everything. I fought my feelings, I fought with myself to make myself see what I was risking losing, an incredible man who I loved and adored and who loved and adored me, why did I have to complicate things?

But I just wasn't ready. My soul, as much I loved him so deeply, my soul kept telling me this is not it. This is not it. And it became very painful because deep down I knew this wasn't it, and I was trying to force something. Until one day, he, always being the strongest one, looked at me in the eyes and said; "Anna, you love me, but you don't choose me."

That hurt so much but it was the truth, and with nothing else left to say, with three beautiful years of memories, and incredible pain in the same heart that was asking me to leave, we eventually went our separate ways.

The loss of P hit me harder than any other loss. In him I had healed a lot of my wounds, I had felt home for the first time and for the first time I had really loved.

To this day, he is the one man that I have on occasion, regretted letting go of. I have much love for him but I know it wasn't the right time, nor lifetime. I still think of him so fondly, and it makes me smile to know that his dream came true, he's happily married and has been given the children he longed for.

I learnt that you may meet your soulmate in this lifetime, but it doesn't necessarily mean that you're meant to be together. That was a really, really painful thing to learn, but I needed to follow my heart, I needed to follow my soul. It became clearer over time.

The Gifts in a Nutshell:

- Relationships can end even when there is real love and that is ok. When on the path of following your heart you will often need to let go of what you love most.
- Staying true to yourself is sometimes the hardest thing when people around you are convinced they know what's right for you.
- Real love never dies, it's just the nature of the relationship which changes.
- Even when all your ex-partners, friends and relatives seem to be getting on with their love life and you don't seem to be, remember, you are living your own journey, according to your unique thumbprint. Live your journey fully and have faith in the knowing that when you blossom, the bee comes.

Please do share with others what you are getting from the book so far. Tell us what lessons you are getting?

Be in with a chance to win a VIP place at one of our Relationships Intensive Event.

Go on share your view:
www.facebook.com/RelationshipsIntensive

CHAPTER TEN

Learning to discoverME

It took me a few months to get over the pain of letting P go, it felt as bad or worse as the pain I had experienced four years earlier through my identity crisis. The pain was so big that at one point I lost my appetite for the first time in my life and lost 10kgs in two weeks. It was remarkable, I reached a point where I didn't want to wake up in the mornings. I resented the sun coming up and then felt guilty because my catholic upbringing had me feel this was blasphemous. I'd then pray for forgiveness and cry in desperation. I felt alone. I had recently set up my business, I had very little income, I would cry in front of the laptop wondering where my next money would come from and I had nowhere to turn to. I had to face this. It was right in the eye of the storm that I felt I heard God speak to me in my ear.

One morning as the sun rose I felt the tightness in my chest as it built up with sadness and anxiety, I did not want to face the day I began to cry and I asked God to help me, help me come out of this hole. Yes I was back in that dark hole but possibly deeper than four years before. And as I lay there face soaked in tears I felt I heard a voice saying in my ear 'Anna, everything is going to be fine, now rise.' It was the strangest sensation but I felt compelled to get up and then a sequence of thoughts came into my mind that were unknown to me. They went something like this: *So long as I'm stuck within myself and my own sadness there will people out there who are not going to see their light. People who are waiting for me to see my light so I can shine for them'* This suddenly gave me a momentary liberation from my circumstance and I realised I had to do something, I had to serve. The next thought that came was an idea, a moment of inspiration and having learnt to follow my heart, and so I did. I remembered that Femi, my ex manager and mentor had gone off alone and set up his own training company, I gave him a call and offered to help. He had a brand new team of tutors and they could do with some guidance. So next thing I knew I was stood in Femi's office, when he looked at me he gasped, 'omg Milena' He'd come to always call me by my middle name as he'd actually learnt how to pronounce it and he asserted that there were two of me, Anna and Milena and he connected more with Milena.

"What happened to you? Even your ass has gone! He exclaimed playing around with me." He made me laugh for the first time in ages. Femi had become like an older brother to me and was one of my best friends, I was safe as I cried in his arms. He also knew P through work and he was saddened by the whole thing. But in that moment, again, I was reminded I wasn't alone and that I had a purpose to fulfill. Femi as always had the wisest words and just such a healing nature about him " Honey, you're going to have to shift focus" He eventually said to me. He was right. I turned out of the office and back into the training room. I ended up working two days a week for Femi for a good part of two years building his team whilst my business began to build up. I loved being in the training room helping others see their light. They say you teach what you need to learn the most. I realised I'm at my happiest when I'm in the training room serving.

For that first year, I was committed to growing out of all the emotional dependencies on men and the compulsion to have to go from one relationship to the next. This was the first year that I spent on my own. I had the most incredible time. I went through the pains of wanting to have someone on a Sunday night to cuddle up with. Yet just pulling through that and saying, "No, I'm not going to find myself someone just because I want to be comforted. I need to learn to be with me."

I was 29 at this point and I was about to have the time of my life as a single person for the first time. It was miraculously the first time that my sister Kucci was single at the same time as me. We felt free to enjoy and connect again like back in the pre marriage days, ahhh.. It was delightful.

One night the whole family was out at a latin bar, uncle George, Tia, my younger bro J and Kucci, we were having a blast. When suddenly I caught sight of a young man sat almost next to me at the bar, dressed angelically in white who was smiling and laughing along with me as I danced in my seat. We got chatting and we instantly connected. His name was Dani but we very quickly decided we'd be cool friends and so we put each other in the cousin box, which we call Primo in Spanish. We hit it off straight away, he was fun and light and within the hour I was introducing him as my primo (cous) to the rest of the family. Who all quickly embraced his animated and fun presence. We exchanged numbers and that was the start of an awesome friendship the beginning of the best summer Kucci and I would ever experience. A few weekends after, Primo invited us to his house for his birthday barbeque. It was hilarious and the best part? We met two of the most awesome single guys out there at the time. That was the night I met my bestie Da Vinci, that was the nickname he inherited in good time because he called me his Monalisa. I also met my dear friend who I called Angelito. That entire summer, every single weekend, a group of at least eight of us, men and women, ALL single, would spend the longest sunny days at the beach, by the river, at a festival or at someone's birthday party. We had the time of our life that summer. I learnt to open my heart to men on a new level, on a platonic, synergistic level. No romance, no desire, just pure friendship and it was exquisite. The hugs were priceless and the connection and love between us grew. These men were all heart centred, open, sensitive, fun and had just so much love for us. We created a sacred space between us and it brought much joy. Mine wasn't summer of 69, it was summer of 2009.

Kucci and I grew a lot from this new found love in male friendship. The synergy relationships we had now created with our friends gave us a lot of freedom and confidence.

Up until that point we'd been very co-dependant in our relationships. So much that during this single period, we'd even set challenges where we weren't allowed to flirt, or communicate with any guy for about a month. It was painfully funny but trained to be emotionally self sufficient, ie, not rely on men for attention and therefore self worth.

As a result we had the most incredible year as single girls. It was about growing and connect-ing with men and women. On a non-sexual basis, on a non-attraction basis. It was just the most beautiful experience. And there were moments where we would cry, because we'd wonder what was wrong with us. 'Why? why have we not found someone.' we'd ask ourselves.   And then we'd just walk through those emotions and thoughts and say: "No, it's just about divine time, and it's not the right time."

Then once the summer was over, I began to have that feeling again. Oh man... Here we go again. Now what? Well it was the feeling that I was getting comfortable and it was time for the next stage of growth. And so now being very aware of the power of personal development and having experienced a few transformational programmes, I was ready to get back in and this time for a longer period and this is when I put myself into a six month leadership programme. I decided, "All right enough is enough of the partying. I need to get my head focused. I need to get my business off the ground." And that is exactly what I did.

Its funny, but it really is the case that whatever you put your focus on manifests. I explained to my friends and to Kucci that I needed to shift focus and therefore things were going to change and they wouldn't see me as often. We still to this day dispute how this episode of our lives came to an end as at the time I hurt DaVinci and Kucci with my choices, but I was really only choosing for me, not against them. It took time. But as with time, everything passes and we'd become even closer through the challenges and joys of our later years.

So I stepped away from the guys and I dived into my business and my leadership training. I felt stronger and more confident than I ever had until that point in my life, it was like I had discovered myself. And so it was no coincidence that within a few months I would attract the opportunity to start up the programme that would change my life and that of many, forever. discoverME.

It was also no coincidence that I would find Mr Drake, a younger man who I would share my next three years with. He was suave, elegant and powerful and together we were a powerhouse. We got together very quickly, we invested together, we travelled and being ahead of me in the growth journey, although younger, he had the communication skills of a true leader. He taught me that we could be one and the power that lies in creating a future to live into. These were great times and we were a rock for one another. It was sexy, it was powerful and it was a real training ground for great communication in relationship.

At the time I was doing some work for an employability provider in the borough of Greenwich called Gllab whilst still working twice a week for Femi, I was enjoying the journey but something major was about to shift.

I designed a programme that incorporated employability training and confidence building for the unemployed. It so happened that on this particular occasion where I was going to be running the programme, Gllab didn't have any space on site so they hired space in a local children's centre. As I walked in, the children's center manager happened to be covering reception that day and she noticed the way the group of people that were going to work with me, walked into the children's centre with their heads drooped, their shoulders down, and looking somewhat depressed. Then she saw them walk out at the end of the day with their chest up, and they were smiling. She stopped me on my way out and said: "Excuse me, Who are you? And what just happened in that room?"

I went over to her and said with a smile, "Hi, my name's Anna Garcia and I run confidence building and employability training for the unemployed." "Oh my god" She exclaimed joyfully, " I want that for my parents! Without the employability bit for now but I definitely want that for my parents here at the children's centre. "Great, let's have a chat." I said. I couldn't believe what was happening. Many, MANY years before, whilst I was a student staying living temporarily near Milend, I used to walk past a children's centre and say, I'd love to work with mums. I'd seen the vision but then completely forgot about it.

Lisa, was the most delightful and beautiful woman I'd met in a long time. We sat down for a meeting and we began to dream out discoverME, it was the beginning of a wonderful partnership and friendship that would last to this day

To this day however, we still debate as to who came up with the name discoverME. But it didn't matter, discoverME was born. We piloted the programme for the first time in September 2009. It was a four week confidence building programme for parents. One day a week. And it was about women learning "Who am I outside of being a mum?" Learning that they are the CEO of their family, the chief ENERGY officer. That wherever their energy was at, their children's energy would be at. That if they love themselves. Their children would also love themselves. That children don't do what you to tell them to do. They become who you are. We began this journey and it gradually spread from children centre to children centre. Then we spread into schools. It was an exceptional journey.

This spread coincided with my soul speaking to me again, this time, around my personal life. As great as Mr Drake was, my soul was telling me this wasn't it either. It was heartbreaking yet again but with such an exceptional human being, the process of recognising the end and winding down the relationship to have it be complete without any suffering was an experience he taught me that I'll never forget and be eternally grateful for. To this day I often miss his example of communication and leadership but again I smile to know that he is now happily married with his very own family.

Spreading into schools and children's centres throughout Tower hamlets meant we helped transform even more families, particularly the more vulnerable ones. One particular case that springs to mind is that of a mum who had mental health issues and was severely depressed. Social services was involved and her children were at risk of being taken away from her. As a result of her participation on the programme, She went from 16 pills a day to 1 pill a day. She dramatically changed her outlook which changed how she went about her daily routine, impacting the children positively. The children were taken off of the register. She got her life back just because she remembered who she really was. 'I discovered ME', she would share with other mums. She just needed to be loved up and like that story, there endless stories.

Four out of every ten of our parents, would end up going into some form of work, training, or education as a result of their participation on the programme. discoverME would go strong for seven whole years whilst parent engagement remained high on the agenda for schools. Headteachers began to see the value of this work for their staff and so we also began to create cutting edge staff Inset days to encourage team connection, responsibility, mindfulness and resilience. Some of my best training days have been staff Inset days.

The Gifts in a Nutshell:

- It's in the eye of the storm where we get to really face ourselves. It's in looking at our pain and sorrow right in the eye that we are then able to transcend to higher levels of love and awareness.
- Only when we learn to be with ourselves, with our pain, our anxiety and our fears can we begin to surrender, stop judging ourselves and begin to discover the greatest love. The love that lies within.
- Living in faith guides us always to the perfect people at the perfect time, or angels as I like to call them. And if we are ready to align and receive their contribution, our whole life can change rapidly in the direction we'd hoped for.
- When we are courageous enough to show up and keep showing up consistently without giving up, we can facilitate a space for people's lives to transform, many people's lives to transform.

- With every step we dare to take despite fear, the more refined our message becomes and with this the more people we are able to reach

Please do share with others what you are getting from the book so far. Tell us where in the world you are reading from and what lessons you are getting?

Be in with a chance to win a VIP place at one of our Relationships Intensive Event.

Go on share your view:
www.facebook.com/RelationshipsIntensive

CHAPTER ELEVEN

Meeting my Kindred Spirit

It was the beginning of 2013. I went out dancing one night with my comadre, the one that saved my life, she came over from Singapore where she was now living with her Canadian husband and 3 children. She was on a short trip and wanted to dance. As I was coming back from a dance this guy came out of nowhere, headed straight for me and asked me to dance. I had never danced with anybody the way I danced with that man that night. I just fell for the dancing. I was like, "Oh my goodness. If this man does anything else the way he dances, I'm in." That was Alex. We danced the night away, and it was just the most beautiful synergy. I was taken by him right away. We knew we were going to be friends. I felt like I'd known him from before.

We got on so well that we agreed to go out the following weekend. We met up to dance and there was this beautiful connection. That night, as we finished dancing, he stole a kiss from me. I said, "Oh no, no, no, you can't do that! This is not what I'm looking for... I just want to be your friend. I would really just love to be your friend." "Why?" he asked with a cheeky grin. "Because I'm after a certain type of guy." "Really?" He said with intrigued eyes, " Well let me find out more. I want to get to know you." He said. Instead of putting him off, my no to him was ammunition.

We went back to my place one evening. I remember we sat on my white, fluffy rug on the floor, in yogi position, knees to knees facing each other. "Tell me, what is it you're after? What is it your heart is after?" He asked so attentively, I said, "Well, I have a dream that I'm going to meet this mature guy. He's a successful entrepreneur and is going to offer me the stability that I long for and encourage me, be my number one fan. And that's why I think we should just be friends". Alex was the same age as me and as amazing as he was, he just didn't have the entrepreneurial qualities I was after in a guy.

And do you know? he completely ignored me. He began to enchant me with his poetry, and his creativity, and his massages, and his dancing. His conversations, we just had the most incredible conversations. About everything, from consciousness, spirituality, the world. We shared the same heritage. So we'd cross from language to language and I hadn't experienced that with anybody for a very, very, very long time. We just crossed. We spoke Spanglish, Spanish, English. And it was just this beautiful chemistry. I really felt he was a kindred spirit.

We began to dance one night and the dance led onto the most beautiful, incredible night ever, the lights, and the mood in the room were just beautiful. All the lights were down and we had passion in our hearts.

The dance became love making. That was the first time we made love, and I'd never experienced love making like that. At the level of self expression, freedom, non-judgment, creativity, romance, and passion all mixed into one. I was completely besotted. I'd never experienced what I experienced that night, with anyone. So precisely the way he danced was the way that he made love to me. It was just like his soul was completely bare. Like we bared our souls that night. It was just incredible. The freedom and self expression. Just total freedom. I'd never felt so free.

That was really the beginning of the most

incredible three and half months of just passion. There were whole weekends, we wouldn't leave the house. For three or four days straight. I discovered a whole new part of me through him. He opened up a part of me that I'd never allowed to come out, and I remember he confronted parts of me that I didn't want to confront. He'd make me say things I didn't want to say to free me from my inhibitions and he brought out the lioness in me. At the age of 33, I began to finally own this passionate woman, this passionate Latina woman for the first time ever. For that I was eternally grateful to him .

But then three and half months in it came to an end and to this day we still debate on who dumped who. To me? I believe that I told him that I loved him, and he freaked out, he said, "I know I'm the inbetween guy, not the right one for you, I know you're waiting for Mr. Right, and you'll dump me the moment you meet him." According to him, he says that I dumped him. To this day we don't agree on that story, but in my eyes, when I told him that I loved him he freaked out. So we parted ways, I remember for the longest time I just mopped around. I missed him so deeply, my soul missed him so deeply. My friends would laugh, "You were only together for three and a half months. What's the big deal?"

The big deal was the connection. It was deep. So instead I just continued to focus on my business and it went on to help transform many, many lives. I completely left Alex to the side. I just forgot all about it. I took him off my social media and my phone. I felt that if I couldn't be with him, I didn't want to have him as a friend either. Strange how I thought then. But I now understand exactly why this had to happen.

The Gifts in a Nutshell:

- Life is like a bus and people come on and off the bus at different stages of our lives. The problem is when we stand at the doorway not letting people off and whilst we do that we are stopping the right people or person from coming onboard.
- Every person that comes into our life comes in for a reason and so long as we remain observant and not attached, we can rejoice in the gems they bring and the growth they offer us.
- When there is love it is possible to part in love, it's not complicated as the world may have you think. Only the ego makes it complicated with its attachments and territorialities
- Our level of consciousness or spiritual evolution will dictate how we are able to transition from a love relationship into friendship. The more ego is attached to the relationship, the less likely is the friendship allowed to blossom post relationship.

Please do share with others what you are getting from the book so far. Tell us where in the world you are reading from and what lessons you are getting?

*Be in with a chance to win a **VIP** place at one of our Relationships Intensive Event.*

Go on share your view:
www.facebook.com/RelationshipsIntensive

CHAPTER TWELVE

Like Bonnie & Clyde; Like Velcro

Tairo was his surname and I loved it. From the moment we met six years earlier at a business event, he stayed in touch, he would always let me know when he was in the UK and asked if we could meet, but I was always abroad or in a relationship and knowing his intentions with me, it didn't feel right to meet whilst I was with someone. Such an exotic man, half Tanzanian, half Polish, how on earth did that happen, right?

This time however, I was single again and on the look out for the man on my list. Yes, the infamous list us women often attach ourselves to that created a space for Tairo to step into my life. It had been six months since Alex and I had parted ways and I was after the successful entrepreneur that lived abroad, that knew what he wanted and meant business in all senses of the word! I wanted to live in several places and not attached to someone all the time, so someone who lived abroad seemed perfect.

He got in touch yet again and this time his insistence seemed flattering and admirable; "Hey, I'm in London, how about we meet up?" And I thought, you know what, what's the worst thing that can happen? I'm single, he's single, and anyway, let's do it for networking purposes! I tried to reason with myself. So I accepted his invitation to go on a date. He booked us a table at a lovely waterside Thai restaurant in London.

As we walked there from the carpark, I noticed how different he was to the average British or Colombian guy I'd ever been with, from the way he walked, talked and carried himself, his accent was distinct and was modest and conservative in his ways. We spoke business from the first moment and that was home for me. Although he excitedly began to 'tick boxes' there was something I couldn't put my finger on and it felt familiar.

As the wine was being served, I couldn't resist finding out why this guy had never given up on us meeting for six years! So I bluntly asked with the cheeky intention of throwing him off; 'Tairo, what do you want?' and without any hesitation he looked me in the eye and said ' I want you'

There it was, the moment he disarmed me, I'd

been the one to be thrown off. You see, all I'd ever wanted to hear and feel from a man was right there with clarity and intention.. pow!

That one date turned into a whole weekend by the coast, it was magical and for the next six weeks of the school summer holidays whilst my business was at its' quietest, we embarked on a journey across the UK in pursuit of his business goals which back then were the very modest beginnings of an empire he would, years later, come to build in his mother country Africa.

We were like Bonnie and Clyde, eyes behind shades and my hands on the wheel whilst he was on the phone negotiating his next deal. We cruised down motorways singing, laughing and bickering and arguing too, yes, he had this extraordinary ability to light my fire and push all my buttons! No day was boring or the same, it was exciting as we went up and down the country sourcing his next car or truck deal. It was like a dream come true, we spoke excitedly about business and I fell in love with his incessant curiosity about everything; my past and my business. He at times, seemed to care more about where I was taking it than I did, it felt great to be supported and believed in. 'You're the next Oprah' he would exclaim! I would respond with; 'And you're the next

Richard Branson of Africa' and we both meant it. We believed in each others' journeys 100%. I knew this man's destiny was huge.

He opened up my mind to the possibility of living and working anywhere in the world, although he lived in a third world country, he was flying in and out of different places like he belonged everywhere, and for that mindset gift, I would become forever grateful to him.

The more time we spent together, the more the familiar feeling would set in however, it was a sense that his heart was troubled. I could feel a deep sadness in him at times and this vulnerability drew me closer.

When his time in the UK was up six weeks later, it was time to say goodbye and as we kissed at the airport he told me he loved me, I couldn't believe it then, but I was later to know this was very true. He was as loyal as they came and his actions later on would be consistent with that.

As I drove back home that sunny afternoon, I couldn't believe I'd grown so attached to someone in such a quick space of time and in that moment I felt that familiar empty feeling. Tears rolled down my face as I tried to make sense of everything that had happened. A date had turned into six weeks of passion, business, fun, antagonistic bickering and did I say much passion? We would bicker, argue and then make love, somewhat like velcro, stuck together and then ripping apart, again and again and again,

Within a few days of him arriving back home he was already proposing plans to fly me out to Tanzania. He was keen to show me his world, introduce me to his family and I was excited to go to a place I'd barely heard the name of.

As I landed in the heat of Dar Es Salaam some weeks later, the 'New York' of Tanzania, Tairo greeted me with a modest embrace and this was the first shock to my system. I had envisioned a whole body experience after a slow motion run! But no, welcome to Tanz, beautifully conservative where public displays of affection are a no-no. We were now in his territory and things here were very different.

It was beautiful, and very soon I would have answers to many of this man's' mysterious ways. You see although our time together was made exhilarating by our velcro like dynamics, most of the time Tairo had a tendency to be elsewhere even when he was right beside me. To start I thought it was his brilliant, laser sharp focus on his business, which I admired, and in part it was, but very soon I saw how absent he could become and how much this would distance me from him.

One afternoon as we walked along the beach promenade engrossed in conversation, I was right in the middle of one of my animated stories, when suddenly he disappeared without a trace. I stood there mesmerised, wondering where he had gone. I knew no one and I didn't know where I was, so I stood still hoping he'd come back from wherever on earth it was he had got to. After some three or four minutes he emerged from a small alley to the side of the promenade and continued to walk as if nothing had happened. I stood still in my tracks and he stopped, looked back and said confused; 'What?'. 'You're kidding right?' I asked in disbelief. 'You really don't think anything of just leaving me mid sentence and disappearing into an alley without saying anything?' 'I just went to the washroom, gosh,' he exclaimed defensively and looked at me like what's the big deal? Oh my goodness, he may aswell have just pulled my hair. He had no idea that it was not only impolite to leave someone talking to themselves, but random to not even let them know that you were going somewhere. This was just the tip of the iceberg when it came to Tairo's randomness and lack of communication. It was alien to him and as much as it became funny in hindsight, it was part of what made us like velcro. We didn't get along in communication at all and this hurt because although it was one of my greatest values, he just struggled to understand it.

Despite feeling like aliens in communication, this trip to Tanzania became a once in a lifetime experience; Tairo intended to give me his absolute best taster of his country, and that he did. We travelled on safari through the extraordinary Lake Manyara, home to an incredible diverse set of landscapes and wildlife. We drove through the incredible Ngorongoro, an inactive and dried up volcanic crater expanding 100 square miles in the stunning area of Arusha, home to many Maasai, the semi- nomadic, colourful tribes that astounded me when I first saw them. We sailed across the Indian Ocean to the breathtaking beaches of the island of Zanzibar, I'd never, ever, seen beaches so white and water so crystalline. We snorkeled in the Indian Ocean, danced under the full moon and enjoyed fresh lobster brought to us by local fishermen. I was in love with Tanzania

Tairo introduced me to his wonderful family who I fell in love with too. His delightful, Polish mother who having lived and worked in Tanzania for over 30 years supporting the Polish community and consulate, was very much loved and recognised within the Tanzanian community. She had this magnetic energy and vitality about her and was Tairo's number one supporter and partner in many of his endeavours. She was taking her annual trip to Poland the following day, so my time with her this time was brief, but it was instant love.

His Dad was deceivingly funny and childlike once I got through his attempt to intimidate me when I first met him. 'Jambo, Habari gani?' He said with a big smile on his face (Swahili for Hello, how are you?) He stared at me, as did Tairo with an 'awkward moment' face. We all knew Dad spoke full English but it was like a stand off! It was like he was waiting for me to break into shyness or something. A very long moment, a moment dad was enjoying fully until I eventually replied: 'Jambo, Im visuri, asante' which translates to hello, I'm well, thank you. I smiled. He exploded in delighted laughter as he looked at his son impressed and pointed at me. 'Ah- look! She speaks Swahili!' and Tairo laughed a sigh of relief. Now, we all knew that was the extent of my Swahili skill, but that was my rite of passage right there! Dad loved me for not backing down and for making an effort.

Little did I know how important that moment of defiance would become in changing the lives of that family forever. I was grateful for all the Swahili practicing I'd done prior to travelling. To be honest, I'd wanted to impress Tairo and deep down was maybe even contemplating the possibility of creating a life with Tairo, but in the end it was daddy Tairo I'd impressed.

Dad and I went on to enjoy the first of many long conversations over tanzanian wine and macadamia nuts and Tairo just watched us bemused. He would reply to his dads' animated questions with the occasional grunt and shoulder shrugging like a resentful teenager would with his head buried in his phone. Dad would tell him off, frustrated at his sons' lack of involvement. Dad and I even danced one night as we exchanged Colombian and Tanzanian traditional moves but there was no turning Tairo away from his phone. And although I disliked his coldness towards his dad, I loved and respected his addiction to business. To me it was admirable. Daddy Tairo just couldn't understand however and this among other things, drew them further and further apart. Dad had dreamt of his son becoming a marketing expert after a degree in the UK but Tairo was an entrepreneur through and through and this caused a lot of tension between them although he was clueless as to why his son was so distant and cold.

One saturday afternoon Tairo left me with dad as we indulged in yet another delightful conversation, he had a business meeting to attend to. An hour or so into our conversation, dad became thoughtful and his tone sad: 'Anna, would you help me to understand my son please?' He said frustrated. 'I feel I've lost him and I don't know why' I looked at this Alpha male who suddenly became like a boy 'Dad, are you sure you want me to help you with this?' 'Yes please' he said with such vulnerability and powerlessness. The truth was, Tairo's love was focused and directed solely to his mother, who he adored, it was wonderful to see but sad to see that dad was kind of left aside and given the cold shoulder. It was strange to have a request like this from such a proud and powerful man, but dad and I had connected over a very short time and I had only love for him despite his edgy, stubborn ways.

'Ok, dad I'm going to be really straight with you, is that ok? I thought I'd ask permission before shooting from the hip 'Yes, please, whatever I do isn't working' He was desperate to understand why his son was so cold and distant. 'Dad' I paused and then said gently 'You don't see your son...'' ''Ah- what do you mean?' he interrupted abruptly in his awesome

Swahili accent.. I stood my ground firmly dismissing his exclamation 'Dad, you are forever insisting that your son become something he is not.' 'What do you mean?' he asked looking so confused. 'Dad...' I took a deep breathe. 'You're son is an ENTREPRENEUR' I pronounced that slowly and firmly. 'Ah- what is this thing, entrepreneur, I hear it all the time? Forgive me, I don't know' He looked lost. 'Dad, it's a saturday night and your son has left his visiting girlfriend from the UK with his dad whilst he goes to do business... Daddy, this boy of yours is passionate about business, it's who he is, it's his number one priority, THAT is an entrepreneur right there. And furthermore daddy, your son is a bloody good one, I know LIKE I KNOW that he will be incredibly successful. But you're missing out because you are stubbornly insisting that he become something he is not. As a result he feels undermined, unappreciated and not gotten.'

I saw in dad's eyes the look of shock, no one spoke to him like that, he was a successful businessman and respected leader in his community, you just don't speak to adults like that in this part of the world. But I came from a space of pure love for that family and for Tairo. And if all hell were to break loose in that moment, I was prepared to take it. Tairo was worth it.

His eyes of shock quickly turned into a euphoric, oh my God, how did I never see this before look. 'Oh my goodness Anna', he said quietly as he gazed at me and then put his head down. He was saddened for having been so stubborn but at the same time excited to finally understand a big part of the reason for his sons' distance towards him. He looked up with an air of excitement and rejuvenation and said; 'Thank you, from tomorrow, everything is going to change, you wait and see, there is much work for us to do together' I smiled with relief.

All the while, Tairo had returned home and had been listening behind the door with tears rolling down his face. Finally someone had got through to his dad, finally his own father might see him for who he is. The following day all three of us went for Sunday Brunch at a hotel by the beach. When I finished enjoying my meal, I excused myself. 'Gentlemen, I believe you have some catching up to do, I'm going to take a walk' and off I went.

That day I walked and explored the beach and surrounding areas for about 3 hours, I was lounging on a sun bed nearby resting my feet and reading a book when they finally emerged. Dad came up to me with tears in his eyes and said 'thank you for giving me my son back' And in that moment everything made sense. I realised what had brought me to Tanzania. It wasn't to start a life with Tairo but to help uncover the root of his sadness, he still had a long way to go, but somehow I knew deep in my heart that I was being used as an instrument. That family dynamic changed forever.

One afternoon as we sailed across to one of the islands, I looked at Tairo as we stood on the deck under the sun, I loved everything about this man, the businessman in him, the son he was to his mother, the loyalty he showed his employees, his relentless go-getter drive, his passion for breaking barriers, including getting together with me after six years across the other side of the ocean.

He was patient, laser focused and incredibly good with numbers. I felt I could build a future with him, I would get excited at the thought of living part time in Tanzania. But there was a big missing. Himself. Tairo had focused his pain and all his energy into business, he had trained so well to numb himself, that he struggled to be present or to connect with anyone in any significant way and this brought tremendous pain to me. I loved everything about him but he wasn't present for me to love him. He was never there, he was lost in his head and had his heart and emotions behind bars. I had never experienced such irony; I was in paradise, with a beautiful man but I had never felt so alone.

In this beautiful moment as the sun shimmered on the water and I had only days to go until my return to the UK, Tairo looked at me and said, 'So..? what do you reckon? Are you going to come and live out here with me in Tanz?' I loved the life, the beaches, weather, private chefs, drivers, house maid, you name it, it was paradise. 'Baby..' I looked at him with so much love for him. And I said: 'I've fallen in love with your country, your people and your family... But I can't fall in love with you' it hurt so much to say it but I refused to lie to myself or to him. I wanted to fall in love with him so badly, I wanted to love him like he'd never allowed himself to be loved but I'd spent the past six weeks trying to love a man whose heart was impenetrable. I was heartbroken and disappointed. How could life bring me such beauty but not allow me to savour it.

That night when we returned to Dar, we walked alongside the local beach and we cried as we brought the three week dream holiday to an end, it wasn't just the three weeks we were ending. I couldn't do this anymore, our relationship had to end as well. For the next year however we'd continue, we'd embody the velcro dynamic. He'd travel 100's of miles to come and see me after a fight to make up, it was passionate, it was powerful and it was incredibly drama filled. Every Time he'd show up at my doorstep to make up I felt loved but what I loved most was telling my best friends how he'd travel across the world to make up. At one point my best friend Da Vinci said 'Omg, you must marry this guy, I mean, who does this kind of thing nowadays, it's incredibly romantic' and yes, it was these kind of comments that fed my ego. I didn't see it at the time but this was an incredibly egoic relationship.

We played the co-dependant- aloof dance again and again and took it in turns to play out each role. When I wanted it he didn't and when he didn't want it, I did. Oh my, it became so dramatic that at some points it reminded me of my abusive relationship in my younger years. In fact, one day I realised it was exactly the same, no physical violence, but emotionally and spiritually it was. And then I came to realise, it was a different face, same energy. What had this man come into my life to teach me if I'd already healed and learnt that lesson?

One day up to my wits end with him insisting we

stay together and showing up unwanted at one of my retreats with my mentor in Malaysia, I was complaining to him about Tairo. Tairo had also become a student to him but I knew full well his trip to Malaysia was about us. My mentor finally said to me. 'Garcia, when are you going to let him go?' I was like 'WHAT?!' 'This man doesn't leave me alone, he shows up at my door, and now he's here!' I defended myself insulted by his suggestion that this was my fault. He went on; 'When you finally let him go, he will let go. But you're causing him to stay around' He said with the calmest, trust me, I know what I'm saying here, tone. Oh that really pissed me off.

I sat on that for weeks back in the UK, I couldn't believe my mentor would suggest this was my fault! And then one day, out of nowhere and for no reason, it just hit me, there it was, the truth hitting me in the face, crystal clear and as bright as day. I was the one bringing him to me. I hated to admit it but I realised in that moment that in my egoic state, his attention and chasing was feeding me and I was getting a massive kick out of it. As much as I was complaining to my friends, I actually deep down loved it! I was disgraced and ashamed. My ego this whole time had taken over. Whilst I was victimising myself and pushing him away, I was fuelling his love for chasing the impossible. It was all very insidious and deceiving.

I began to pray and meditate and I finally made the conscious decision that I would set him free. We spoke on the phone and I took responsibility for my actions, I owned up to my nastiness and I apologised. 'Tairo, I'm so sorry, I've been a bitch and I'm responsible for the amount of pain and suffering I have caused us. I love you and I let you go.' There were tears for many days to come as I released the Tanzanian dream and grieved the love and the possibility of what may have been but it was the right thing to do. I thank God for my mentor in that moment for having the light to show me what my ego didn't want me to see and what no one else saw.

It took several years before Tairo and I got in touch again and today we are good friends. I'm privileged to share about our journeys over a phone call. He's a great role model and he thanks me for the gifts I brought him and his family. His laser sharp focus paid off and he is well on his way to building his African empire.

The Gifts in a Nutshell:

- No matter how evolved you are, if you allow yourself to react to somebody else's ego patterns, you are at the effect of your ego in that moment too.
- We will attract partners that will invite us to heal the parts of us we haven't healed yet, so don't resent your partner!
- Whenever ego kicks in in the relationship it's not the end of the world, it's just life showing you what you are now ready to heal, but it's up to you whether you use the opportunity to transcend.
- When someone is not leaving, even when you've been asking them to, consider there is a part of you that is unconsciously holding them back, there is something your ego is getting from the whole dynamic or drama.
- Many couples become unconsciously addicted to the ups and downs of emotional drama and pain and think its normal. Society teaches us this but this is not true of real love.
- If Love is turning to hate or resentment at

the flick of a button, it begs the question,
is this real love?

....

What do you get from these lessons for yourself?

*Please do share. Tell us where in the world you
are reading from and be in with a chance to win
a **VIP** place at one of our Relationships
Intensive Events.*

*Go on share your view:
www.facebook.com/RelationshipsIntensive*

CHAPTER THIRTEEN

Meeting my Mentor

It was January 2014 I was having a conversation with my best friend Arzu, I explained to her, that I'd got to the point in my business where I didn't know where I was going next, I didn't know if I was doing it right or wrong or how I could make it better. I'd had enough. And I said to her "I need to find something, and I've done everything, but I need to find something different to guide me" She continued to explain to me that a friend in common that we had, a very successful girlfriend who was doing really well has being doing something called Wilson Luna. I'm like, "who?" She continues to explain, "oh it's this mentor that she has, and she goes to his events and whatnot." And I said, "Well, let me check him out."

I went online, checked him out. He had a free event coming up that weekend, and I said, "oh what are the likes of that." I showed up to his room, there were hundreds of people there and within 15 minutes I knew I was home. He was this extremely...How to describe someone who's so extroverted ... He was just, he just really didn't give a f**k. He used the word f**k every ten seconds. He's this crazy Australian Latino guy. Very, very successful entrepreneur. Just wanted to teach young entrepreneurs Well, wanted to teach small businesses, business, and he was just an incredibly enlightened human being. I had not seen a speaker like that in such a long time. I don't think I'd ever come across anyone like that. He was bold, shot from the hip and full of love.

I just felt like it was someone who could understand me, someone who I connected with immediately. So needless to say, I signed up to his programme, and that was the beginning of the most incredible last three years to now. Very, very quickly, he was able to identify what my business was about. He was able to show me and guide me and say, "Anna, keep doing what you're doing." For about six months, "Keep doing what you're doing." And he just built me up with so much confidence. I was reassured that I was on the right path. I was reassured that I was going to go somewhere, that I was going to make a difference. He had a massive belief in me that no one had ever had, no one. He just had a belief in me.

He changed my world, and he said, "young lady, your life is about to change completely... " He paused, stared into space to absorb what he said and said it again, your life is about to change completely, you have no idea." Within six months he challenged me, and he said, "You're going to need to change everything about your business," I was confronted, I was crying, I was upset. He completely invited me to remodel my whole business, and I began to do that. I went from working within schools on a small group basis, to running large events one to mass, so that I could reach people. And I was so petrified, because I'd never considered doing that. He said, "You're ripping people off by not doing this. You want to reach lots of people? make a big business? This is the way forward."

So that's what I began to do. Kicking, screaming, umming and ah-ing. But I did it, you know, and it's now been two years since I began to do one to mass with his guidance. I've traveled the world with some of my best friends following him around on quarterly retreats, this training became vital in my growth as a facilitator and as a business woman. I was no longer the same person. He opened up my world in ways that I'd never ever imagined. I met an incredible network of souls that he'd brought together through his programme that I'd only dreamt about. They became like family, half of them live in Australia and half of them are in the UK. We just built the most incredible network of entrepreneurs. It's now been three years, and it took discoverME to where it took it within the funding cycle time that it had. discoverME is now coming to an end.

And this is where Relationships Intensive (RI) was born. About two years ago, in Sydney, Wilson comes up to me after an event, puts his arm around my shoulder and says super excitedly; 'Omg, I've got a fantastic idea about what you're doing next Garcia!". Everytime he called me Garcia it was like he was pulling my hair, I felt like a soldier. he started calling me by my surname about a year into our journey. I now know he did it because he knew I still had stuff around my surname. There was a subtle undercurrent that I didn't realise still about my paternity and it was that I carry the Garcia name so proudly but underneath there was a discomfort because I have it that I'm not supposed to be a Garcia. Wilson is wise beyond this world and he sees things lightyears ahead of when I do.

"This is what I see you doing Garcia. Given all the experiences that you have, I really see you in this arena... It's freaking HUGE and you're the best person for it." I couldn't believe what he was saying to me, didn't he see how many relationships I'd gone through and failed at, surely a relationship specialist should be married and such? They should have a much neater relationship CV than mine? I tried to reason with him but he would answer 'Don't you see, this is precisely why you're perfect for this! Today relationships are different, people are desperate for a new message and model about relationships and this is the message you bring, I know it'

Everything I had ever followed this man on had turned into miracles and gold up until that point so I chose again to open my heart and allow myself to be led in faith. It took some time, about a year and a half in fact before I finally came to him and said; " I'm ready Coach" " Ahh Garcia, this is f**king music to my ears" " You have no idea how huge this is going to be, the world needs this message"

He had the patience of a saint. I was ready to start this journey but if I'm brutally honest, I hadn't a clue what I was going to be doing, I just knew I was ready and kept moving forward, doing as I was being guided. It was like going through the woods with google maps, Wilson was my GPS. I just trusted and had faith in his vision and belief in me. What I did know for sure however, is that I wanted to impact as many lives as possible in as little time.

November 2016 saw the first RI programme. That first time on stage, I looked at one hundred and forty plus women, most of whom were my network and friends of friends and I said to them; "This didn't happen overnight ladies, please know, this you see today has taken fourteen years." Everyone clapped in celebration and I really trust they got a valuable lesson out of that.

It took me five RI events and four advanced weekend courses (RIA) before the penny really dropped for me. This was the moment I aligned with my message, I surrendered to God and I remembered fully that I was only here to serve.

With this, I lost all fear and became unapologetic about my programme, my message and my delivery. It was then that I stepped onto that stage and I said, God, just speak through me, whatever these ladies need to hear, let me be your channel. And so it was. I got myself out of the way and spoke with love and bold, unapologetic compassion. I made it very clear that I was going to add so much value to them through showing them WHAT they were doing in their relationships and WHY they were doing it, giving them a glimpse into the 95% undercurrent that is running the show and causing the results they have. But that if they were ready to transform their life, let go of the past, stand in their sovereignty and create relationships they love from a clean canvas, then I could show them how to in the advanced programme.

That day we had record registrations onto the Advanced Programme. Women aligned with the clarity, the peace and the power I emanated, this is what I later heard them say. I confirmed then, it's all in the being. People don't buy into your product or service, they buy into you. When they see in you what they are longing for in themselves.

I was so grateful that I followed blindly, you know, I just trusted, I had faith. It was when I ran my first advanced program with a small group of women that were totally committed to having massive breakthroughs around their relationships that I realized, this is what I was born to do. This is why I came here. And it almost felt like my soul had arrived somewhere. It was like it had jumped on a horse, and the horse turned round and looked at me and said, "Anna, for goodness sake, finally you're here.

Now, the journey is just started now, let's get going," And like in the beginning of any worthwhile journey, it stretched me in ways that I never could have imagined. To suddenly be dealing with the public and managing events, event organizing, filling up rooms and reaching out to women, some of them that who are in a lot of pain. Some of them that reject you outwardly, openly, overtly. But I had to learn, It's not about me, and it's about trying to get this message out to as many women as possible. That's now my journey. It's taken something. It's confronted areas of me I didn't know I had and shedding ego in ways that I never knew possible.

One of them is just the letting go of people's opinions of me. That's a huge one. Being fully self-expressed in my message, and knowing and being okay with the fact that a lot of people are not going to like me, and a lot of people are not going to agree with my message. But being true to my message so that those that do align with it, can be lit up. And that's been the journey with my mentor. I'm incredibly grateful, because he sees me and he sees through to what I cannot see. But I know that the last three years would never have happened if I hadn't crossed his path. It's been the most magical thing, and I thank God every day, every day that there are people like him, who are out there, living to their full expression so that others can do the same too.

Today Relationships Intensive runs as a one day event once every six weeks or so and it's a powerful introduction session, a taster to what is possible on the advanced programme. The ladies who come along get so much value, they learn about themselves in relationships and leave empowered and with faith in themselves again. Those that go VIP love it even more because they get to spend extra time with me in a private group session and get their specific question answered.

Those that then choose to join the advanced programme have breakthroughs in their relationships they never imagined possible. Women who have held resentments their whole life with their dads, mums or relatives learn how to let it go for good. One young woman was stuck in her relationship of many years because she couldn't get over having had an abortion, she was resenting her partner and filled with guilt. She was able to finally free herself from this guilt and the resentment and this brought a whole new life to her relationship which is now blossoming again.

Wilson once said to me; " Garcia, just become and the world will see you, it will come to you.''

Recently I was speaking at one of my best friends' events. Gozi, who holds a wonderful event called soul summit brought her mentor along to speak. I'd heard Warren Ryan was going to be there and having heard such wonderful things about him I was excited and admittedly, a little nervous. This guy trains people to speak, a leading mindset coach, international speaker and founder of the Fearless Speaking Academy. I'd never been officially trained to speak, I just grew into it. So, of course I was a little nervous! But after sharing with my dear friend and fellow speaker Taran who was also speaking that night, I chose to let it go and just went on stage and did what I do best, be me.

That evening, Warren spoke last and I tell you, I was blown away, brought to tears and felt like I'd been resuscitated. He poured love, passion and life into my heart for speaking again and I thanked God for giving him the courage to shine so bright and give others permission to do so. That night as we said goodnight, he thanked me for speaking to his heart and telling him what he needed to hear. I told him, that I was the one that was incredibly grateful. He doesn't know it, but my life changed that night. I was going through so many changes and at times feeling lost and he brought me right back to why I was doing what I was doing and how best to do it.

When you shine your light you eventually allow yourself to be seen by those matching your vibration. The connection with Warren was instant as we both came from the same place in serving the world and speaking, we came from the heart. It was like finding your long lost twin! It was great to find someone on the same path, wanting to create a dent in the universe and coming from such a space of love. It was inevitable; we had to work together.

Today I am blessed to speak internationally, I share the stage with some of the UK's top speakers and leaders in their field. I have partnered with Warren Ryan, international speaker and mindset coach and we have a schedule of exciting events coming up including a Relationship & Connection Retreat in Thailand. I will also be sharing the stage later this year with the amazing Chris Hill, addiction specialist who's causing massive impact in the world with his work worldwide. It's a blessing and a privilege to be surrounded by extra-ordinary human beings who have just taken their painful past and made it into the brightest flame to light the world. And you can do the same to.

The Gifts in a Nutshell:

- When the student is ready, the teacher will appear.
- Sometimes you need to follow in blind faith and the bridge will build underneath your feet as you go
- When you act in faith and consistently, you cannot help but create results and change your life
- When you just focus on becoming, the right people will see and come to you. Become and the bee comes.
- Sometimes you may really doubt yourself, that's ok, just keep going, they're just thoughts and beliefs coming up. Each day you can press the reset button and start again
- When you stand in wanting to serve from the heart everything unfolds naturally
- Patience really is a virtue and will keep the dream alive when times get tough. Have compassion with yourself and be patient. Not Rome nor you were built in a day.

Please do share with others what you are getting from the book so far. Tell us where in the world you are reading from and what lessons you are getting?

*Be in with a chance to win a **VIP** place at one of our Relationships Intensive Event.*

Go on share your view:
www.facebook.com/RelationshipsIntensive

CHAPTER FOURTEEN

Big Brother; Childhood Bully to Hero

As a kid my relationship with my older brother G was very dominant-submissive, I was annoying and he was a bit of a bully. He's six years older than me and I felt somewhat controlled by him. I often felt powerless around him and as a result over the years I developed fear of my brother. I didn't feel that I could just approach him or call him or reach out to him. Until life pushed me to back in 2003, with my paternity issue.

Life always intended for us to get close but our fear and our pride kept pushing us away after the events were over. The only thing that kept us close was my relationship to my sister in law who I love dearly and the gift she and my brother gave me and the family, my niece and nephew, Sadie and Frankie. These kids changed my world when they arrived and I had the privilege of having a very trusting sister in Law, she would let me take them for the day since they were tiny. Sadie was only six months when I took her with me for the first time and then Frankie was born less than a couple of years later. They were completely different characters and I loved embracing each of them. The word auntie had a whole new meaning to me. When I ask Frank who is my favourite boy in the world, he confidently says: 'I am'. And when I ask them who is luckiest, them or myself? Sadie confidently replies; "you're the lucky one auntie". These cheeky monkeys were the only reason I kept insisting on a relationship with my brother. There were times over the years where I tired of his distance and aloofness and I wanted to give up on trying to connect and have a relationship, but I couldn't not be a part of those kids' lives. And I vowed to myself that I would always be in their lives and have their back regardless.

At the time in my life where I enjoyed great connection and relationships with everyone around me, I'd given up on ever having a close relationship with my older brother. But life had other plans; life knew I needed to transcend this one. So life spoke out loud again and brought us together for what was set to be the longest time ever.

After fourteen years, sadly, my brothers marriage came to an end. When he came to tell me, I was saddened but I'm his sister and I'll aways be there for him: "Well, whatever you need bro. If you need to leave and you need to come and live with me, whenever you're ready I am too." I knew how different my brother and I were, and I was a bit nervous, but we did it anyway. Eventually my brother moved in. Little did I know that I was about to face my 'nemesis'. I was about to live with the person that, I guess, made me feel the most nervous. The person that took me right back to childhood, no matter how much work I'd done on myself, how much I'd grown, how much of a leader I was in my work, in my community, in my family.

When it came to my big brother, I felt completely dominated and I was in my own home. Completely back into my childhood patterns where I felt I had to tread on eggshells around him. I always felt I wasn't good enough. In his aloofness I felt rejected and whilst he spent a lot of time in his head minding his own business, I was saddened by the lack of connection and by my concern for what he thought of me, or didn't! It was exhausting.

I knew this was all in my head and there was a big reason why at this point in my life, my big bro had been sent my way. My brother was indeed a really cool guy, minding his own business, very busy and yes, often in his head but I'd also noticed he had grown much more sensitive and caring since having his children.

As a result of all of this mental and emotional exhaustion, I was somewhat miserable at home, I felt suffocated.

Until one day I sat down with him and I said: "I cannot believe that at this point in my life, you're the one person who's opinion I worry about. You're the one person who, if I were ever to fail in my career, I'd be worried about. You know, you're the one person that I struggle to connect with."

He looked at me, he had tears in his eyes, and he said, "I'm so sorry, I am so, so sorry. I know you and I have always been so different and we struggle to connect, I find it so hard to talk with you too." Then he said, "You know, I'm committed for us to change things." he said, "And know that, we're no longer those kids Sis. I mean, really see me for who I am today." He pleaded softly. I suddenly had a big reality check. "I know, I really am going to work on that." I said. I realised I was holding onto a childhood image of my brother and living as if it were happening today. In that moment I gave up all expectations and demands I was making of my brother and I breathed again. Who am I to make demands on someone, to expect them to be anything other than who they are? I realised my suffering came from expecting my brother to be with me a different way and not just let him be and love him for who he is and for who he isn't. It was so freeing.

Life wanted me to heal the biggest childhood wound I had, the seeking and never finding of validation and approval from my older brother. And life had it's own way of doing that, it gave me the opportunity to be there for my brother, and for my niece and nephew who I adore. It just allowed us a space to create so much synergy between us.

I've gone through stretching times since with the growth and changes to the business. When I've had my moments of doubt, I've looked towards him, and said, "Please tell me. If you didn''t think that I should be doing this, would you tell me?" He answered: "Oh my God, of course I would tell you." He's the most practical, pragmatic guy that I know. He turned round to me and said: "This is who you are, and I wouldn't see you doing anything else. You must keep doing what you're doing."

To me in that moment, I fell in love with my brother all over again, and every day he just became my hero. Through my ups and my downs throughout. He is just there, and he's that person that I can count on to just be so emotionally neutral and I've learnt from him. Up until that point, my brother and I had never really been able to connect, because I had it that we were just so different. I'm a right brainer, he's a left brainer. I'm a daring entrepreneur, he's a top CEO for a multinational company, he has a secure job, has the kids. He did everything by the book, and I did everything so completely differently.

Then here we were, both in our vulnerabilities, in the middle of life not showing up where either of us had planned. We just sat there in front of each other and saw who we really were, there was just pure love. Who my brother is for me today? He's a hero. Someone I can seriously count on. Today he's moved into his new place and I've followed him temporarily. I'm grateful we have been given the chance to be a team, to be connected, to finally have synergy.

The Gifts in a Nutshell:

- When you drop your expectations and stop making demands on your loved ones, you give them the space to be who they are and to be loved for who they are. Ask yourself, 'who am I to make demands on you'
- Learn to love people for who they are and for who they are not it will change your life.
- When dealing with someone inclined to be aloof , dominant or co-dependant, mirror their level of connection without clinging, dominating or becoming aloof yourself. Just bring love, remove judgment and be present. Stand in your sovereignty, knowing that you are whole and complete just the way you are and so are they.
- Being present with someone means giving up your ideas about them based on the past. They are no longer that person if you allow them.
- People will love you their way, be open to receive it or you will miss out whilst trying

to change them.

Please do share with others what you are getting from the book so far. Tell us where in the world you are reading from and what lessons you are getting?

Be in with a chance to win a VIP place at one of our Relationships Intensive Event.

Go on share your view:
www.facebook.com/RelationshipsIntensive

CHAPTER FIFTEEN

My Soul Brother

I was eight years old when J was born. "Mummy, he looks like ET". Was the first thing I said when I went to meet him at the hospital, poor mum. I have a special connection with every one of my brothers. My eldest one is my hero, the youngest one is my baby. And J is my Godson.

From the moment J was born, I always had nightmares about losing him, about dropping him. I always had such a sense of responsibility for him, and I never understood why. As we grew up, as kids, we were like cat and mouse, we were always fighting. But I always felt, like I was incredibly responsible for him.

In 2007 I explored Peru as part of my travels, whilst in Machu Picchu, my besties and travel buddies Arzu & Ndidi, inspired by my spiritual adventures in Colombia wanted to have "an experience" and so one of the guides recommended we go visit a priestess of inca descent during our stay in Cusco. As we drove up in the taxi she was at the doorway, 'I've been expecting you' How was she to know what time we would get there? We certainly didn't.

Her name was Gladis, she invited us in and asked us to sit around a table. I sat in between the girls as my role was simply to translate. The girls wanted an experience and they were certainly about to get one. Gladis was a descendant of the Incas, and could read you, your past lives and then some. She was very mysterious. She brought out a plastic carrier bag and spilled cocoa leaves (as in cocaine) over the table. We were about to get a reading that would change our lives forever.

After translating for the two girls I was in shock as to how accurate she was about things that only we knew. I had no plans to get mine read as I felt I'd had enough spiritual experiences that summer to last me a lifetime but after witnessing this woman's abilities I had to ask if she could read mine. She agreed. As she threw them on the table and formed a circle with them, she instantly spotted the incident with my dad. She said, "Oh wow, your dad; I can see here that your paternity shifts." Then immediately she said, "What's this with your younger brother?" I was surprised but my heart leapt, "Yes, PLEASE tell me about my younger brother." Up until then I'd been desperate to understand why the feeling of guilt ever since he was born; I was 8 years old, what could I possibly feel guilty about. " You have such a sense of responsibility for this boy." She said with a serious tone. " It's Like, there's this huge pain that you have with him." "Yes, I feel guilty." I said "I feel guilty when it comes to him, I almost feel like I have to compensate. I always gave him far too much, I always felt like I owed him."

"Well, first of all welcome home." She said and she paused as she looked at me with a warm smile and so much love in her eyes. "What do you mean welcome home?" I asked. "Yes, welcome home… you were an Inca Princess!" I said, "what are you talking about?" Suddenly I recalled a moment I lived only a few days back whilst in Machu Picchu. I'd sat on some stairs among the ruins overlooking the mountain range ahead. I just stared into these mountains and began to cry my eyes out. Not knowing why the heck I was crying, but I just felt like I had to cry, I was so moved. I was alone for about two hours, just staring out to the mountains, just crying and crying and crying.

"It was the time of the Spanish inquisition." She interrupted my thoughts. "And you know, some things never change, Anna." She commented with a touch of irony; "You knew you were about to be taken by their leader and so you chose to throw yourself off that mountain instead. You prefered to die than to surrender to a Spanish Prince," She looked at me, she grinned and said, "Some Things never change, right?"

"And now here is the answer to the question you have always had inside you... Your brother... He sadly witnessed your death. He cried your death his whole life. He never got over it because you are soulmates. You have travelled together through many lives as partners, lovers and siblings..."

I couldn't believe what she was saying but it made so much sense, it brought immense peace to my heart. Whether this was true or not, I opted to believe it because it gave me an empowering context for our relationship. There was more though: "and that is why, from the moment he was born, you feel indebted to him. and that's why, in that debt you feel that you owe him. In this lifetime you are his guardian, and you chose to be like a guardian for him. That's why, you say you're his Godmother right?"

He was a young teen when he asked me if I would be his Godmother for his confirmation.

My heart leapt when he asked me and now I understand why it was such a powerful moment. "That's why and you're going to be such a right-hand for him"

And that was absolutely true. Within a couple of years, J, who had remained in Colombia with my mum, was knocking at my door in London, and he stayed with me through college up until when he went to Uni. I was like his second mum, and for many, many, many years after that. Every time he finished term at uni, went back to uni, I was the one that would drive him back and forth from bournemouth with his stuff. For the longest time I was his bank account, taxi driver, advisor and confidant.

Until eventually I realised that through my guilt, I was incapacitating him. I was doing him no good. It was such a pivotal moment in my relationship with my brother. He'd finished Uni and he was just in a kind of limbo. I was facilitating life far too much for him. All out of my guilt. What guilt? It was just an unreasonable guilt. And I said, "Enough. I am not going to be responsible for ruining this young man's life," because I knew that was what I was eventually going to do. I was making life too easy for him and therefore robbing him of the chance to build his name, his life.

So I sat him down one day and I said, "Amor, you know I love you more than I love most people on this planet. But as long as I continue to facilitate this, your life is not going to get any better". So my brother left. It broke my heart when he went back home. But I'm forever grateful; after several years of coming and going between the two countries and finishing off his studies he eventually settled in Colombia, where his heart always was. Today, J as well as working with me from a distance, he runs a successful business with his beautiful partner Paula, she's drop dead gorgeous and a powerhouse when it comes to family and business. They share a beautiful life with their dog Simon and I'm just so freaking proud of him.

Today I get on with my brother really well and we are a team, but it did take me all my twenties and a lot of suffering to come to understand him and the way he loves. When he was living with me, I lived with so much pain. I would sometimes cry myself to sleep because I literally had it that my brother didn't love me. As much love as I gave him, I wanted to hug him, I wanted to kiss him. I wanted to tell him that I loved him. My brother could never express the same back to me. I'd ask him, "What is it? Why do you treat me like this?" His non reactive response was always: "What? I'm not doing anything." And it was true.

Little did I know then that it was just my brother's way of relating, the aloof way. He had no need for seeking approval of others. He had no need to hug, to kiss, it just wasn't his love language. The only time I get a hug from J is when I land in Colombia, when he picks me up at the airport. And I get a big hug and I get three pats on the back, one, two, three, let go. Then I'll get another hug on the way back. But he doesn't do touching, it's just not his love language.

In fact what I learnt later on, when I bothered to look into it, was that my brother was someone who enjoyed quality time instead. He'd enjoy being with me, and we didn't even have to be talking, in fact, I came to learn that the less I spoke, the better. No hugging, kissing, none of that. It' wasn't his love language. But he very quickly learnt what my main love language was. Acts of service. And so if I asked him to do something for me, he'd done it yesterday. That's the way he expresses his love to me.

J was a massive lesson in learning to love people for who they are, then you know you are free. I learned that my brother was never going to love me the way that I wanted to be loved. That wasn't his job. My job on the other hand was to appreciate the way that he knew how to love, the way that he loved to be loved, and to love him for what he was and for who he was.

For me, it was such an alleviation when I finally realised I could just love people how they love to be loved and not insist on being loved the way that I want to be loved. And that was big for me.

The Gifts in a Nutshell:

- We often project our fears onto our loved ones and we may overprotect them or do 'anything' to see them happy. We don't realise however that we are incapacitating them and not allowing them to build their own muscles or shine for themselves
- When we let go of guilt we can come from a space of love and compassion. And compassion isn't always pretty, it can be tough, blunt and direct.
- When we really love someone we let them free, we encourage them to be the best version of who they are even if that takes them away from us.
- Suffering leaves when we embrace people for who they are and don't expect them to change to fit into our model of the world.

Please do share with others what you are getting from the book so far. Tell us where in the world you are reading from and what lessons you are getting?

*Be in with a chance to win a **VIP** place at one of our Relationships Intensive Event.*

Go on share your view:
www.facebook.com/RelationshipsIntensive

CHAPTER SIXTEEN

Like Brother, Like Son, My Son-brother

When I was pregnant, I was anticipating my mum to travel to the UK to support me when I gave birth. Then halfway through my pregnancy she called: "Princess, I've got good news and I've got bad news. The bad news is I'm not going to be able to travel over to you" my heart broke. "The good news is I'm pregnant too." Oh my God. I could not believe it. There I am, at 18 years of age, pregnant, and my mother is 40, on the other side of the world, and pregnant too. It was just the most surreal thing.

After I lost my child, I travelled home to be with my mum. She was heavily pregnant. I took her a card which had a beautiful baby on the front, blonde with blue eyes, there was no reason for me to suspect that my baby brother was going to be born with beautiful blond hair and blue eyes. But he was. He was the most beautiful baby I'd ever seen, but I didn't get to meet him until a whole year later. When they decided to migrate back to London. I still remember the first time I saw him as they came through the airport, he was sat on the suitcases on the trolley, my heart leapt with love and joy, oh my God, this was the cutest bundle of joy I had ever laid my eyes on.

And to have him come and form part of my life at this precise time was the most healing and welcomed experience. As Brandon grew up, I was like a second mum to him. I'd dance with him to make him fall asleep. I'd carry him around with me everywhere, he was just the most adorable, adorable child. They eventually traveled back in 2006, leaving the biggest dent in my heart and my world but mums heart was always back home.

Brandon was about nine years old by this point and our relationship never changed with distance, in fact it grew stronger. One day he contacted me "Nena, I would love some help with an assignment" I'd become his Nena since he learnt to speak. We'd arranged to speak the following day.

That following morning, I was in meditation. And in my meditation I saw a view of my living room, and in it I saw Brandon, my God daughter, Lorena and my daughter. They're all roughly the same age and they were playing together in my living room. In my meditation I saw this. The following day, when I spoke to Brandon, he said to me, "Oh my God Nena I had the weirdest dream with you last night." Now remember there's a six hour difference, so while I was meditating he was asleep. He said, "I was in your home in London, and I was playing with Lorena and then this little girl came out of nowhere, and she had a gift in her hand, and it was for you."

In that moment I realized the level of connection I had with my brother. While I was meditating I saw the three of them. He had no idea who this little girl was. But when I told my mum she had shivers, I can't believe it. Brandon's not even aware, he's too young to be aware of the story of his niece. Yet that was the kind of connection that we had.

He has since lived in Colombia and every year I go out there and I love hanging out with him. We just have the most synergistic relationship. Brandon and I come together, and there is no competition, there is no codependence, there is no domination. It just pure Synergy. I feel whole and complete in his presence and it's just such a privilege to have him as my brother.

In recent months Brandon has found his calling

in tattooing. He is gifted. So after attempting university courses and realising it just wasn't for him, he began to study and train in tattooing by some of the leading tattooists in Colombia. His dream was to travel back to the UK to pursue his art here and so he did. As apprehensive as we all were about him abandoning a professional career and travelling back to the UK away from his mum, he's been met only with miracles which I take as a sign that he's on the right path. He is being mentored by a leading tattooist in Camden Road, works in a bar part time, has joined a music band and crews at my events. One could say he is living 'the life', of an eighteen year old in London at least!

We spend quality time together when we can and he's a real support at my events. the other day I just stared at him, my eyes watered and I said; "You know, I really was worried about you coming to this country. But I now realize that we've been put on each others' paths again so we can serve each other and others better." He smiled and as always said " I love you Nena"

I talk about the 4 types of relationships at my events and they're such an insight for people. I feel blessed that I get to experience them all through my brothers! Whether we choose to be Aloof, co-dependant, Dominant-Submissive or

Synergistic, there's no right or wrong. It's just acknowledging that everybody has their flavour, their hangout place. The biggest thing for me with my brothers has been to come from loving them for who they are, and for who they're not. And the same goes for my parents as well. Learning to love them for who they are and for who they are not. And that has given me so much freedom, furthermore, who do I wish to be for them? That's just been such a freeing experience.

The Gifts in a Nutshell:

- Life will always give you the gift of synergistic relationships if you are open to them. Nurture and value them, they are gold in a world where relationships are becoming increasingly difficult
- The child we lose remains our child forever if we keep the connection alive even if it is limited to the spiritual realm.
- The most precious gifts from life are unexpected. You still don't know what amazing people are still to be born or be drawn into your life. How exciting.
- Everything that happens no matter how sad or hard has a gift in it if you are willing to see it. Sooner or later the gift will appear.

Please do share with others what you are getting from the book so far. Tell us where in the world you are reading from and what lessons you are getting?

Be in with a chance to win a VIP place at one of our Relationships Intensive Event.

Go on share your view:
www.facebook.com/RelationshipsIntensive

CHAPTER SEVENTEEN

Kissed By An Angel

I met up one saturday afternoon with a speaker friend of mine who lives abroad. We were having dinner and this great conversation about what we would love in terms of relationships. "Anna, so what's the deal with you?" He asked. "You know what? I'm happy as I am. I giggled. I'm really cool and, you know, one day maybe the perfect guy will come along. But right now I'm just happy, I'm just enjoying the relationship with myself, with my life, with my career."

He looked at me and said, "I would love to create someone, and I'm struggling to do this... I would love to create someone that I can connect with, that I can make love with, that I can just be with. That I can just...you know? But I don't want to label it, I realize that I've not been creating what I want because I have this idea that I have to create a full blown relationship and all these things that come with it." There was such profound truth and resonance in what he was saying. As he continued to share, it sang so true in every part of my visceral body, I had tears coming to my face.

I said, "Oh my god, buddy you have no idea what you've just said to me." He said to me, "What do you mean?" I said, "You've just described and articulated what my soul has just resonated with. I would love someone that I can connect with, that I can feel a true, true connection on all levels. That I can have incredible intimacy with, and that can just be free to explore without having to limit it with any "relationship label" oh my God, I was just so exhilarated, and he was just laughing. "Thank you, thank you, you have no idea. Thank you." I so gratefully exclaimed to him. "It's like I now know what I want to create, right now." He laughed "All right, great, well I'm glad I was of help!" He said a little astounded with my breakthrough.

That night I didn't walk to the car park, I skipped! That night I was talking to my cousin, and I said, "Oh my God, I just had this massive breakthrough. I realized that I don't want a full blown relationship and stuff right now, because I'm just focused on my career and everything, but I really would love intimacy, I want something so powerful and something that doesn't need labels, something that's just right."

Suddenly, this thought comes to my head. Alex. I wonder how Alex is doing?

Alex, my kindred spirit , the lover that brought out the lover in me four and a half years ago. Why on earth did he just come to my mind, I hadn't thought of him in years. Do you know, I wonder how this guy's doing? "Hey Alex how are you doing? long time." I wrote him a message. And surprisingly, within seconds he replied: "I am so well, how are you?" He was so excited to hear from me, "I would love to meet with you." He said. "Great. But I tell you what, I'm so busy over the next few weeks, it would have to be either tonight or in two and a half weeks."

"You know what, I'm just finishing work now, I can make my way there. Where are you living?" And it was like that, within forty minutes he rocks up at my house. As he walked in through my door, it's as if he'd never left my life. And the connection was immediately there. It was a new man who walked through the door, time had served him well. He was hundred times more confident, secure in himself, stable, everything that I love in a guy, oozed out of him.

We began to catch up on old times and suddenly he did it again, he just kissed me. It was like going back four and a half years, except it wasn't. We were two very different human beings that had grown up so much. He said, "you do remember that promise we made to each other." I said, "Really, what's that? He says, "We promised each other that if we weren't married by the time we were 40, we'll just hook up." And I said, "I can't believe you remember that, I'd forgotten that completely. Oh my god that's binding." And he said, "Well we're 36 now, what do you reckon we give this another go?" I smiled, I loved what I was hearing but I had to stay true to what my heart wanted. I said, " you know what? Right now, all I want is just to connect. I just want to love, be loved and let's see what happens." he said: " you know what? I'm totally up for that."

It just so happened that we were both single, we were both ready to connect and we were both in the same space. That was the beginning of that, little did I know, that Alex would become the most incredible rock, and a support for me throughout this incredible journey of growth that I've been on, in regards to Relationships Intensive for the best part of six months. He hugged me that first night and said; "I know that you're such a powerful person, you're supporting so many people, but I know deep down there's a little girl that just wants to be loved, and wants to be held, and wants to be protected. And I want to be that for you." And he kissed me and I literally felt like I'd been kissed by an angel. My heart melted and he didn't see in the dark that it brought a tear to my eye.

Although I was happy and content within myself and my life he awoke my physical need for oneness. Our physical body will always be one half of the whole, the female or the male and together they make one. This is why we have the urge to come together and the act of sex is the most heightened experience of wholeness we can achieve in the physical plane, hence why we are so attracted to the opposite sex.

In that moment all the concerns that I had about the type of guy that I thought I was going to end up with, or the type of guy that I wanted, It just vanished into thin air, it just no longer mattered, we found connection and we didn't have any labels around it. It was exclusive, I kept saying to him, "you're my Mr. Right Now and I'm your Miss Right Now and let's see what happens."

"I really like him" said G, my older brother, as I sat one day to chat with my new found confidant. I said to him, "You know, he's not the alpha male, sleek, successful guy that I'm supposed to be going out with" Oh my god, it took me right back to one of the exercises that we do in the advanced program, How will I allow you to love me? And it's essentially, how do I want to be loved. I'd made this list a few months before Alex came on the scene, and I brought it out; I went through this list and pretty much everything that was on there, Alex was loving me that way. "Do you know what," I said: "Tell me how do you want to be loved?" What a great question to ask a lover. I'd never known intimacy the way that I knew it with him. How exposed I felt a lot of the time, vulnerable. And I'm not talking sexually necessarily, I'm talking in conversation, the depth that he was willing to go into with me.

I felt like I'd been kissed by an angel.

And for the first time in my life, It wasn't about, is he the one? is he the one I'm going to marry? Is he the one that I'm going to have children with? It was just about, this is who I am with right now and it feels so darn good.

We were approaching half a year together and life and business began to change dramatically. As the need to seek stability increased I began to project it onto Alex. I began to crave his company to soothe the pains of growth and I began to feel the pains of attachment. Yup, I began to get attached! Like a drug when he was with me I felt complete and when he wasn't I felt empty, and this was what I'd always aimed to grow out of from previous relationship patterns. Codependence! This wasn't going to serve me or my journey so I began to pray to God for discernment. Then there it was again, yes, you guessed it, that feeling that it was time to move on.

In seeking God I finally accepted the invitation by one of my best friends Lili. Every year she'd invite me on a silent retreat run by a catholic nun but I'd always been too busy or too distracted. The thought of spending three days in silence horrified me, but I'd had enough of running my relationships on attachments. So this time I went. I checked in at the convent where it was being held, it was so peaceful. We were a small group of women and we were each shown to our rooms. It was all very simple and perfect. Each morning I would meet with Sister Ruby and she would give me some bible passages to study throughout the day and meditate on. The idea was that I would read, meditate and then just sit and listen. They were beautiful grounds and I spent different parts of the day in a different room or garden area. And this is when it began to shift for me. I felt like I was going home. I had some of the most beautiful conversations and as I listened I was reminded of who I was and all I needed to be. " Be love" I heard " Stay close to me and let me take this". Up until that point I thought I'd stayed close to God but I realised I was really trying to go it alone. I felt great relief to remember I didn't have to. In my conversations with God I was shown an image that I was a branch that had broken off the tree and drying up. This represented me being away from God, from source, whatever you wish to call it is really irrelevant hear. I quickly created an image in my mind, heart and on paper of growing back from the tree as a brand new branch. And I felt alive again. I was also told that life needs two things, focus and flavour. Too much focus without flavour causes density and sadness and too much flavour without focus causes anxiety and lostness. "Honey, I heard God say, you hang out in too much focus for long periods of time drying your soul up and then retaliate in to flavour bringing distractions to self-sabotage. It's time to bring focus and flavour. I found so much peace and love, I was home. I asked for clarity in my message to the world and it was given to me. "Hija mia" , which translates to child of mine in spanish, "Your message is so clear, and he proceeded to tell me exactly what it was, which I summarise into three points:

1) Pinpoint and Let go of any guilt and resentment holding you back and release it. Free yourself from the past and create a clean slate for your relationship
2) Free yourself from any anxiety in your relationship by knowing and building confidence in who you are and how you want to be loved.
3) Learn how to go into synergy and get your sovereignty back in your relationships so you can stand present, centres and naturally irresistible as a result.

I couldn't believe that God was giving me the answer to a question I'd had since starting Relationships Intensive which was; How exactly do I let these ladies know what I can do for them? And there it was in these three points. It rang so true and made my whole body vibrate. I was in ecstasy with the power behind those words. They describe exactly what happens on the advanced course. Not only had I found immense peace this weekend, but I even got guided with my message to the world. This was an incredible surprise yet today I figure, why should it be a surprise? If this is my mission on earth, surely guidance is always to hand. I just hadn't been ASKING for it.

I vowed that weekend to stay close to home and to live as a branch on that tree called home, God, with focus AND flavour. The Next RI event saw our record number of ladies registering onto the advanced programme and the life changing transformations were epic.

My energy began to shift. I'd prayed for detachment and this was showing up everywhere, my brother was leaving for his new place, my dearest cousin who had lived with me for many years was leaving and discoverME was starting to see its' final days. It was time to move and fast.

This can often seem confusing to some people, but I've come to understand 'the feeling' and its' purpose. It's' a feeling that guides us all on our unique journey. We all have an inner GPS. I've just become devoted to paying attention to it now.

I came to have a lot of love for Alex, but for the next leg of the journey I was embarking on, I needed to travel light. So with pain, but more love and gratitude, we decided to shift from our lovers' egoic relationship into friendship and today this one breathes synergy. No attachment, no clinging; just a celebration of love & will when we come together.

Although painful, these changes now come more and more naturally to me. Contrary to what most of society believes, I believe relationships can have sell-by dates. People used to vow to stay together forever because back then 'forever' met the average life expectancy of 50 years. Today we have a life expectancy of over 100 years. My observation is, even if I married at 50, that's 50 years by one person's side. I absolutely salute those who believe in forever and I have much respect for those relationships but personally I have no expectation as to whether or when I will create a 'forever' relationship.

I've come to learn that most relationships are flawed, unless the individuals who form that relationship are in a love frequency or vibration, i.e; Being love. What I mean by this is that relationships aren't love, WE are love. But to really be love is living away from attachments, jealousy, territoriality and addictions. And I realise that most of us operate from here, not love.

My choice of 'being with me' right now as opposed to in an intimate relationship with someone else, is not out of a lack of opportunities, but out of a choice to stand true to my heart and my journey which wishes to fly, to soar and to serve the world.

In longing to be loved from the outside I brought much suffering to my life. Today I understand and wish to share with you that your happiness and your future are no longer hanging on the status of a relationship but rather on your ability to self love, own your story and know who you are.

When the flower blossoms the bee comes.

May you Blossom and Become

The Gifts in a Nutshell:

- When we allow ourselves to create connections beyond the constraints placed by society's notions of relationships, we become free to love.
- Just because it doesn't make sense to anybody else, it doesn't mean you shouldn't go for it.
- You have an internal GPS, trust and ensure to use it
- Life needs two things; Focus and Flavour, or FLAVA! If we are too heavy without flava we become heavy and sad and if we are too focused on flave, we lose direction and feel lost
- The bigger the journey you are on, the lighter you'll need to travel. So expect to live a much more detached life; leaving behind people and things that may weigh you down.
- When you shine bright, the world will see you. You Show up everyday and the world begins to see you. The flower blossoms and then the bee comes. Blossom and become.

Please do share with others what you are getting from the book so far. Tell us where in the world you are reading from and what lessons you are getting?

*Be in with a chance to win a **VIP** place at one of our Relationships Intensive Event.*

Go on share your view:
www.facebook.com/RelationshipsIntensive

About The Author

Anna Garcia is a relationship specialist dedicated to the transformation of women through their relationships.

A facilitator and speaker for over 14 years, Anna shares in her first book, her compelling life story that personally and professionally prepared her for the journey in the world of speaking & relationships

Founder of The Relationships Intensive, the ever growing, popular and life changing programme for women.

With powerful gems to be grabbed from her tear jerking, as well as hilarious stories, Anna shares life-changing lessons that have touched the lives of many through her work

Also, the founder of discoverME, the confidence and relationship building programme for parents which has been running for 7 years, Anna continues her work within the education setting, transforming the lives of children's families through the empowerment of mothers.

Anna continues to live in London & continually grows her work to better impact women by collaborating with other great speakers & facilitators worldwide

Find out more about Anna and her Relationships Intensive Programme at
www.relationshipsintensive.com

NOTES.

NOTES.

NOTES.

19377948R00129

Printed in Poland
by Amazon Fulfillment
Poland Sp. z o.o., Wrocław